D0561196

HOW ARE YOU?

Connection in a Virtual Age

*A Therapist, a Pandemic,
and Stories about Coping with Life*

Therese Rosenblatt, PhD

RosettaBooks®

NEW YORK 2021

How Are You? Connection in a Virtual Age: A Therapist,
a Pandemic, and Stories about Coping with Life

Copyright © 2021 by Therese Rosenblatt

All rights reserved. No part of this book may be used
or reproduced in any form or by any electronic or
mechanical means, including information storage and
retrieval systems, without permission in writing from
the publisher. For information, please contact
RosettaBooks at marketing@rosettabooks.com.

First edition published 2021 by RosettaBooks

Cover design by Lon Kirschner

ISBN-13 (print): 978-0-7953-5315-4
ISBN-13 (ebook): 978-0-7953-5316-1

Library of Congress Control Number: 2021938493

RosettaBooks®
www.RosettaBooks.com
Printed in The United States of America

CONTENTS

CHAPTER ONE

A New Context: What Kind of F*ckery Is This?   1

A New Clinical Situation   13

CHAPTER TWO

How the Pandemic Intensified Existing Needs and Introduced New Challenges in Therapy   19

Challenges That People Had Before the Virus Were Accentuated as New and Different Pressures Arose   23

Coping with Loss and Grief   30

Loneliness and Isolation   33

Overcrowding, Cabin Fever, and New Tensions, as the Balance Was Thrown Off in Relationships Between Family Members and Other People Living Together   40

Parents With Young Children Were Overwhelmed   49

The Separation Process for Young Adults Became Complicated   52

Heightened Struggles With Substance Use   59

People Did Not Have Their Usual Solutions and Supports   60

An Open-Ended Timetable Exacerbated All These Challenges   64

CHAPTER THREE

Refreshed Approaches to Therapy (and My Own
Personal Evolution)   67

The Elastic Frame   78

Billing and Email   80

Session Length, Predictability, and Endings   81

There's No Office Anymore   85

Remote Therapy   90

Therapy by Phone   92

Therapy by Video   104

Virtual Work Takes Its Toll on the Therapist   113

The New Landscape of Self-Disclosure   118

Use of the Self and Personal Theories   131

CHAPTER FOUR

Virtual Therapy (Really!) Works but Doesn't Substitute for
In-Person. What's the Balance?   149

CHAPTER FIVE

How Are We? . . . Where Are We and Where Are We Going
Post-Pandemic?   159

Epilogue   171

CHAPTER ONE

A New Context: What Kind of F*ckery Is This?

ow are you? I rarely heard those three words in my work as a therapist before the pandemic. For close to a year, every single patient started their session this way. How the world changed for my patients and for me. We lived through a societal crisis together on a grand scale. The deep impact of this shared experience changed the very nature of my work—from how I conduct therapy, to the way I navigate the traditional boundaries between therapist and patient, the pandemic shook up the old order of things forever. I was challenged to rethink my practices—how I apply the analytical disciplines, theoretical framework, and theories of my rigorous training.

The pandemic transformed my work, starting with my patients' first words. *How are you?* Pre-pandemic, patients normally plunged right into their own stories, as is the long-standing custom of therapy sessions. During the pandemic, my patients wanted to know how I was first. How was I weathering the storm? As much as we were living through a global trauma collectively, we were, each one of us, also alone. So many of our norms were challenged and rethought, both at the personal and the societal level. My patients knew that I was facing many of the same seismic shifts as they are. When they asked me, "How are you?" I wondered how I should answer.

I am not a therapist who likes to answer a question with silence. Yet I did not want a session to stray too far into personal territory, which can delay or obstruct the therapeutic benefits of focusing on a patient's experience. Pre-pandemic, I might have said, "Fine, thanks." Polite. Perfunctory. Then I would have listened for what the question meant to the patient. In the early days of the pandemic, I often answered more fully: "Hanging in there," or "Okay," even, "Fine," if it was a day when I felt good. Then, as in before times, I listened for what the question really meant to my patient that day. As the months accumulated, I began to revert to my old answer and say, "Fine." For a new reason: when I heard my patients' voices, I was happy to be with them. I was *fine*. I felt privileged to do this work; to share space with my patients grounds me. Our lived experience of our world is now divided between pre-pandemic and the emerging post-pandemic.

The pandemic has caused a radical and unprecedented revolution in our lifestyles and behavioral patterns. Amy Winehouse's lyrics from "Me and Mr. Jones" often run through my head. *What kind of fuckery is this?* Our approaches to life, work, and love have changed in ways that will last. For many of us, during the pandemic, we tried to tell ourselves we were fine, but

We were not allowing our true feeling to be in the forefront of our minds. The pandemic was a crisis. We were so flooded with feelings and new information that we couldn't even put our full response into words. In the midst of a crisis, we are most focused on managing daily life, not processing what's happening to us. We are, to a certain degree, dissociated. We may feel out of control, overwhelmed, and possibly even numb. Like other collective crises, we will likely always remember where we were and what we were doing when we first really took in the news that there was a pandemic. I've been following reports of lethal viruses around the world for a long time and had long feared we were overdue for a pandemic. When I first read the news from Wuhan in late January, I was terrified. I felt overwhelmed and helpless. Then I numbed out and told myself it was okay. But just a month later, on the phone with a colleague, trying to organize an in-person meeting for a group of us, when my colleague said, "We need to take this new virus seriously," I suddenly realized that everything was about to change. The effects of a threat to our well-being last long after the initial danger is over. You are a different person than you were at the beginning of 2020. The way I live and the way I work are altered for the long term.

As we faced the cataclysmic impact of the pandemic, many of my patients openly grieved their losses. Some were overwhelmed, almost to the breaking point, by the pressures imposed on them.

Nancy found herself homeschooling her four children, in addition to building her new business and maintaining the household. Some were cranky and angry about the irretrievable indignities foisted on them. Teresa and Frank could not be with their elderly parents as they suffered their last days of the pandemic in the hospital. Teresa is a neurologist, so this was a double offense for her. One of her core characteristics is that of a caretaker. She prides herself in being there for people and gets especially deep satisfaction out of accompanying people in the gritty, hard, existentially threatening moments. Teresa said goodbye to her mother over the phone. There's a hole in her spirit.

Some were delighted that the solitude they've always loved, which had set them apart from others pre-pandemic, was not only sanctioned, but advantageous. Betsy was so relieved about the decrease in social demands. I myself delighted in having more time to myself and with myself. I very much enjoy my own company and always have a long to-do list for pleasure, work, and projects. I developed a newfound friendship, a close and compassionate relationship . . . with myself. I indulged my interests and love of solitude in ways I had never done in the past. Others discovered or rediscovered their most basic priorities in life. Emma realized she didn't need to go to the theater. Ken, Kevin, and Elizabeth all strengthened their resolve to separate from the home fires and forge their adult lives. Some rebelled by flouting the rules of social distancing and mask wearing.

Our emotions rolled through us, and still do, as we struggle to make sense of the last many months. One day we feel fine; the next we are battling with the subterranean rumble of despair. Our reactions came in phases during the pandemic. Initially, many felt optimism and energy. I did. After all, how long can a pandemic last? A year? Two years at the very most, like the 1918–1919 Spanish flu pandemic. I was primed to take this on ao a challenge and determined to be positive and adaptive. Then a phase of weariness set in. Social distancing and hygiene were essential and will likely be some part of our precautionary practice going forward. They take energy. Melancholy lurked right around the corner. The pandemic was not a hoax. The pandemic was a living nightmare. This is the nature of trauma. Survival mechanisms allow us to feel some level of *matter-of-fact*, some remove, when we are experiencing the utter helplessness caused by traumatic events. It is only afterward, now, that we feel the full force of the impact, that we recognize how we are altered and scarred.

I was in survival mode. We emerge slowly from this mentality. At times I feel positive and can-do. In the first months of the pandemic, I had the happy experience that my husband and I bonded more as a couple. For a period, one son and his wife lived with us. My other two sons came home more often, and my connection with my husband loosened again to include them, an altered happy circumstance. Some days, I felt demoralized and scared. At bedtime, I have always felt some separation anxiety, a resistance to leaving the world for the night. That anxiety was more pointed during our isolation. I looked for more distraction in the evening. I fought against sleep. Then there were evenings of an enervating exhaustion. My body felt hollowed out, filled with the entire weight of the pandemic, plus all the other contemporaneous disasters, political, racial, and environmental. Most often, I felt two things at once. There was no either-or. Nothing was binary. We were and still are filled with contradictory feelings. For quite a while I fought off the blueness. Then the blues were unavoidably present. Decades of experience working with patients in therapy has taught me that no good comes of locking out negative feelings for more than a short time.

Even our sense of time changed, became less precise. It was difficult for me and others to mark time. There were fewer appointments outside our house or bubble, fewer distinctions between the days. Only my work schedule kept me grounded and tied to a reassuring sense of the concreteness of time and place (as opposed to cyberspace). Friends and patients reported that they were experiencing the same phenomenon. In his book *Man's Search for Meaning*, about life in Auschwitz, Victor E. Frankel wrote that, in Auschwitz, days lasted forever, but the weeks flew by. The end of many pandemic days surprised me with their small gift of extra time. While the pandemic was certainly not akin to the Holocaust (though, for some, I recognize that it was a terrible time), I quote Frankel because his words are resonant for the form of captivity we endured.

Some people talk about this being a lost year. This is not at all my experience. Nor is it the experience of many of the people I interact with, patients, family, and friends. People, myself included, are living intensely, but differently. Even those who are suffering are living. Who says that life is only life when things are going well? Who says that we only live when we are out and about? Suffering is an intense form of living, just not a form we would ever choose.

My living this year has taken place within a smaller circumference than pre-pandemic, but it has been no less full and meaningful. I have reveled in my house. My work with patients has been rich and profound. I have written this book. I have deepened my relationships with a smaller group of family and friends. One son married. Another got engaged. Another formed a close and loving relationship with a woman he had just met prior to COVID. Two of these sons started wonderful new jobs, and the third son polished his abilities in his existing job and is applying to grad school. I could go on, but you get the picture. And last and possibly the most fruitful meaning I have enjoyed, my internal life and growth have flourished especially in the opportunity afforded by the absence of my past freneticism.

Seven months into the pandemic, I walked into my New York City apartment and into a time warp. I'd left the apartment five and a half months earlier for my house in the suburbs. Pre-pandemic, I was about to put that suburban house on the market. I thought that part of my life was obsolete. My children were grown and gone. I could return to the city. Everything in my apartment was exactly as I left it, beautiful to my eyes. I spent seventeen years in the suburbs and never felt at home. I waited all those years to get back to this apartment and my beloved city. The apartment was a petrified forest, my closet a museum of times past. I picked up a few items to bring back to my house. I wondered whether my clothes will come alive again when the pandemic releases its spell. I love clothes and fashion. I feel pangs of loss. Will my clothes even be relevant or fashionable when the pandemic and recovery are over? For me, clothes have always offered artistic ways we can transform ourselves, even if temporarily. And now?

Just as our feelings rolled through us in cycles during the pandemic, the period of recovery and the return of a new and altered "normal" will impact each of us differently. Some will respond by unleashing their pent-up emotions in a new Roaring Twenties frenzy of social activity, of wearing stilettos and sequins for a Tuesday night movie. Others will be more conservative and will want to wear nothing but sneakers and their pandemic-comfy clothes. Yet others will suffer long-term wounds.

I love clothes too much to give up the creativity of fashion forever. At the same time, I value comfort more than I did before. My relationship with clothes has evolved and will continue to evolve as we move into the uncertainty of a post-pandemic world.

Now in the twelfth month of the pandemic, the wheel has turned again. I feel and hear from others, a kind of pandemic weariness that is more severe in its tone than ever before. It is different from the weariness I felt before the pandemic. It is the weariness one feels from too much rest and inactivity, from the too-little stimulation that comes from sameness, being a homebody and from yielding to the regression of not putting on one's public face.

The past year of sheltering in place has been like a long hibernation. Even though I have been working (a lot) throughout it all, it has been sublimely restful to work from home, to not commute, travel or oscillate between homes. It is only now that I am feeling the first very faint stirrings of wanting to emerge from my cave, to even imagine putting on full makeup and going to my office. I sense a slight restlessness, at times, a rekindling of my wanderlust. My much-loved travelogues have been calling out to me. I suddenly want to get a mani-pedi. The thawing of this deep sense of hibernated rest illuminates the extent of my past mental fatigue that I had never before realized, especially since I was mostly aware of having high energy. How stretched was I? What kind of toll did this running around exact from me? How will I be different as I emerge into the new world?

What I do know is that we are all in this together, therapists and patients alike, this pandemic and this period of recovery. Everyone. Looking out for others' well-being is as important as caring for our own. We all need and deserve each other's empathy. Coincident with the pandemic, we faced unprecedented protests and riots, plus accelerating environmental devastation that may have complicated or intensified our reactions to the pandemic. These events happened without adequate leadership, accentuating our feelings of aloneness and bewilderment.

At the beginning of the pandemic and concurrent cluster of worsening events, I hoped that we would rise, fully, as a society, to the call of these circumstances to care for one another. Pundits were talking about the need for more empathy in leadership. Political candidates used words like *love*, modeling empathy. Or so it seemed. We had a unique opportunity to become a more empathic society. We could have used this pandemic to reduce the flagrant narcissism that is so prevalent. With the new Biden-Harris election, we have a shot at it. But the Capitol insurrection, the prevalence of conspiracy theorists and millions of voters who believe that the Democratic victory was illegal make the work an uphill battle. The jury is out.

I had hoped that one of the shifts we would experience in response to the pandemic (and the Black Lives Matter protests, plus devastating wildfires sparked by climate change) was that empathy would be recognized as a critical factor in leadership, in politics, and in policy formation. The historian Doris Kearns Goodwin wrote that President Lincoln's success as a leader and unifier was due to in large part to his prodigious empathy and ability to relate to the suffering of the average American.

We elected President Biden partially on the basis of his well-recognized empathy. I am waiting to see if his humanity will have a healing effect and influence the sensibilities of the American public. I am hopeful.

The strain of extreme anti-empathy in the Trump administration sparked new conversations. That administration's shocking disregard for the suffering and needs of others inspired more people to talk about empathy and take it seriously as a concept. The election of Joe Biden signifies a move in this direction. Is the country's choice of a new leader a seed that will find fertile ground, or will it fail to germinate? In my work, for the first time during the pandemic, I felt compelled to talk about politics with select patients, because to not do so would have been to ignore the real impact of the unprecedented situation on all our psyches. Politics as usual was no longer the norm. In meeting my patients where they were psychically, I acknowledged that their political angst reflected the reality in which we were all living. Only then could and should I relate it to the particularities of their unconscious, if and when that was relevant to that patient. I'll say more about this later.

Traditionally, Americans have been wary of so-called soft concepts like empathy, understanding without judgment, love, soul, and even passion. This suspiciousness can extend to the kind of therapy that I practice—psychoanalytic therapy—which deals with the dynamic unconscious and its dominant influence over our conscious behavior, thinking, and feeling.

My work is rooted in psychoanalytic therapy, which is the foundation of all talk therapy. Founded by Sigmund Freud, it offers a consistent, disciplined framework for our work. Sadly, in the US, in many ways, Freud's discipline had been turned into a cartoon of its original intent. The rigor was misinterpreted as cold and distant. People unfamiliar with the nuances of our work imagine a therapist with horns, who makes their patients lie on a couch without looking at them, rarely speaking to the patient. In the comic book versions of the practice, the work can be heartless and unresponsive to the patient; few work in this way anymore, and only a few ever did. Over the past decades, there have been many humanizing changes. While it is true that there are restrictive aspects to the practice of psychoanalytic therapy, the core and true spirit of the work is a life-affirming human interaction. Freud's own patients would travel to Vienna, spending months with him, occasionally sharing meals with him. The work, as he practiced it, is, in fact, highly creative and emotional, which is exactly why we need such precise ethical parameters.

This sensitive work can get risky when we are mucking around in people's hearts and minds. The potential to harm people is real. To protect against that possibility, Freud spoke out against what he called wild analysis. A good analytic therapist practices with a great sense of responsibility and a do-no-harm ethic. Our conservatism and restraint are baked into our discipline.

Over the past few decades, the field of analytic therapy has actively discussed (and argued about) how to modify and open up our discipline, so that the training is perceived as less of a straitjacket. There have been numerous discussions, papers, books, and presentations from a theoretical and clinical standpoint about how we can adapt the work by admitting more of the human aspects of ourselves into the work of therapy. I am personally exploring how we can cultivate more intentional warmth within the evolving parameters of our discipline.

I am also a very disciplined person, which is perhaps one of the things that drew me to psychoanalysis in the first place. I tend to be a strict rule follower with a heavy conscience. So I bring to my practice the heritage of psychoanalysis, heightened by my own tendency toward rigor. I have always believed that this is the best way to offer serious therapy.

Yet my barriers have eased. Even before the pandemic, I had become convinced of the need to bring more artistry and more of the therapist's *self* into the work. The pandemic has tripped the last tumbler, unlocking the final permission I needed to unleash my creativity. Going forward, my charge is to find fresh ways within the enduring analytic framework to offer therapeutic change that enlists more of my intuition, creativity, and humanness. In other words, more empathy.

I hope that empathy, which is at the foundation of good therapy, will be appreciated as a value in the wider world and in our most intimate relationships. The world is ready for such change. The foundations are shaken. I am reinventing myself in my work and in my life. My colleagues feel this impulse toward change, too.

This book is a chronicle of what it was like to practice therapy in the time of the contemporary pandemic that COVID is—the challenges I encountered during this strange and unique time in history, as well as my observations of both my patients and my own reactions. Then I will delve into the practical details and nuances of how the therapist's craft needed to change and will continue to change. Wrapped up in these shifts is my own evolution as a therapist and as a person. Preserving the therapist's unique role as interpreter of the unconscious is a constant in my work. The ways in which we can be helpful in that role require rethinking, even transformation. Threaded through the professional and societal narrative in this book are the personal details of how the pandemic unleashed a new creativity and artistry in my work. I was on the runway pointed toward a new way of working before the pandemic. During the pandemic, I took off. Now I have no intention of landing anytime soon.

I will share my ideas and suggestions for ways to navigate the positive and negative impacts, as well as the potential long-term shifts that will inform our practices for years to come. My ideas, of course, are all filtered through the lens of my own personal reflections on our new reality and how I am changing, personally and professionally.

Of course, this book is not just about therapy. After all, life and therapy cannot be separated, because therapy is nothing if not a profoundly human endeavor. Here, on the other side of this pandemic, is a world transformed. In these pages, I want to share what I'm seeing of our future through my patients, my practice, and my life.

A New Clinical Situation

The therapy profession had to deal with the twin issues of a real medical threat and the advent of exclusively remote sessions. Carol initially brought up the possibility of taking a walk together for our sessions, but we never did. She was either uninterested or at least avoidant of the topic she had raised. Eleven months after the start of the pandemic, none of my colleagues were seeing patients in person yet, either. Patients and therapists alike are impacted by these massive shifts. Can we therapists fill the role of partner in crisis and post-crisis recovery and be a guide at the same time? This is our new challenge. To be more of a partner to our patients than we have been in the past, yet still being our patients' guides down into their unconscious. We must accommodate their practical issues, even as we have to integrate those realities into the analytic work of the unconscious.

As never before, we need to *come up to the surface* at times, to meet our patients where they are. We need to find the new balance between surfacing and diving down into the less conscious layers whenever possible. We need to learn to parse the real from the psychic, in a new way, to respect what is concrete or literal, a category that has taken on a whole new importance and context than it did before the pandemic. Like working with people who are dealing with the very real privations and insults caused by physical illness, old age, and poverty, the pandemic made the *real world* more present in every therapy session. The work of therapy can potentially be richer and deeper as it acquires an intense edge, forged by the extraordinary conditions of this crisis we share with our patients and which will reverberate for some years beyond the end of the pandemic. Like those who lived through the Great Depression, we who lived through the pandemic will be forever imprinted by its urgency.

I experienced an increased sense of intimacy with virtually all my patients, as we adapted and moved forward together through the crisis, as just two real people.

I felt and continue to feel a pull to discuss practical matters with patients. Sometimes I talk with them about what I think of as a *we* matter. That is, challenges we all face. Other times, the practical point of discussion is a *you* matter, pertaining specifically to that patient. Practical can be appropriate, especially during the pandemic and the recovery period. At the same time, I still believe that we therapists must be parsimonious about it. The practical discussions I engage meet patients where they are. These conversations are how I learn where the patient is when we are not sharing the same physical space. As I listen to the details of their everyday living, I hear their unconscious, too.

Because what did not change about being an analytic therapist is holding all these different threads in our minds—the real, the unconscious, all that connects them, and the many theoretical and personalized lenses and techniques available in the discipline of psychoanalytic therapy. These threads are an abiding distinguishing characteristic of psychoanalysis. Our major goal in psychoanalytic therapy is to get to the meaning of things.

Here, before I mention my first patient session, I want to clarify that throughout the book I will tell my patients' stories in the present tense, to preserve the immediacy of their experiences in the moment and in our sessions together.

Finn has a serious chronic disease. After a prolonged lull, he is now spending more time in our sessions talking about his illness, his medication, and his treatment. While his disease is under control, our work together is helping him to see what the illness means to him. In his family of origin, illness was covered up. A flaw was something to be hidden from the world. He was different from the rest of his large family. During the pandemic, though we spent more time on the daily depredations and concerns of his illness, we continue, too, to mine the deeper layers of his psyche.

In addition to the practical talk, I more frequently feel an urge to interpret sooner, make more self-disclosures and answer questions more directly. Is this a pull to a more active stance? Is it a diminution of impulse control or a need to affirm that I am present and engaged, a longtime proclivity of mine that I have always tempered with the conscious use of the technique of abstinence? I will explore all these questions in this book.

What I know for sure is that I am working harder to create a communication bridge. When there is silence in our virtual connection, I feel the need to know if the patient is there and okay. The chitchat can at times establish connections and an environment of safety, from which a patient can reach her own inner life. I have also found, especially during a phone session, that my talking to a patient who is having difficulty talking herself can jump-start the patient into making contact with her own narrative and discussing that out loud.

Although silence has always been an enormously important component of psychoanalytic therapy, I now need to be more vigilant about monitoring the border between a productive silence, that the therapist is best advised not to interrupt, versus a silence that leaves the patient feeling lost, abandoned, deadened. My role is to try to understand the silence rather than thoughtlessly making it go away.

In general, I am listening more acutely. Some of this is to make up for the lack of visual cues on the phone, but some is to make up for the loss of a palpable human presence even on video—their energy, the psychic touch of our physical proximity.

I am working harder, too, because I worry that a patient's ability to free-associate is constrained and inhibited by the current that they are swimming against. Free association was Freud's fundamental rule of psychoanalysis. The idea that patients must follow their thoughts out loud, without censorship or judgment. When the patient feels safe and held by someone trusted (their therapist), their defenses can soften and make way for a rich trove of material from their previously inaccessible inner life. But their defenses might go back up if the patient feels like their therapist has withdrawn from them in some way. Unless this process is discussed and understood by the therapist and patient together, it can hinder therapy. The move to virtual therapy feels like a withdrawal to some, but certainly not all, of my patients.

The technical challenges of virtual therapy exacerbate whatever propensities patients may have around trusting that I am present for them and that I remember and care for them. The virtual world can provoke and surface any insecurities that we (patients and therapists) harbor around our basic ability to relate and bond to others and, even more importantly, another's ability to bond to us. I am alert to interactions with patients that lead to unexamined enactments and mutual resistances around these insecurities, a dynamic that may be implicit or disguised as technical or practical issues. This concern is complicated for those patients who require more distance. To further complicate matters, those same patients often long for more intimacy in relationships, even as they also require distance to bolster their psychological comfort. A productive therapy is not necessarily measured by the yardstick of intimacy.

As much as I am focusing intently on my patients, I find myself slipping into analytical reveries more often as I try to sort through the changing circumstances. Am I talking too much?

Not enough? What do I do in the silences? It is harder now to judge whether a silence is productive to preserve or whether the patient is in trouble and needs to hear my voice. In my experience, I know that I can say a lot without saying much, provide a space filler, if I think the patient needs to feel my presence and I am not yet ready to make an interpretation or ask a question. But I sense my own anxiety in our new virtual environment. When I'm in the room with a patient, I have cues, both conscious and unconscious, to interpret the nuances, so that I can guide, comfort, and regulate us both. I am not yet regulated in my role as a remote analyst in times of great upheaval. I am learning and adapting. And even as I am acclimating to the new context, I am alive and present to this transformative moment in my patients' lives, my own, and the world's.

CHAPTER TWO

How the Pandemic Intensified Existing Needs and Introduced New Challenges in Therapy

Depression, anxiety, hopelessness, and helplessness are just a few of the pandemic's effects. As never before, I experienced the same challenging circumstances right alongside my patients. At first, I felt optimistic. Then, as we discovered that the pandemic would not end anytime soon, and we had no one at the helm to guide us to relative safety, I experienced a first wave of negative feelings. I observed in myself and others how the low moods were followed by positive adjustments. These cycles will stretch well beyond the pandemic's immediate threat. There are periods when we recognize and appreciate the silver linings offered by the pandemic—the freedom of working from home, not commuting, a precious windfall of family connection, quiet, increased time in nature, and more. Avowed city dwellers (like myself) lost their taste for the city and now hanker for greener attractions.

This is a permanent change of attitude for me. The discovery of something delightful and life affirming is unlikely to go away. We reap the calming effect of nature, the optimism of a front-row seat to enjoy nature's beautiful show, to witness the life cycle close up. For me, when my city, New York, no longer offered contact with the people I love and the abundance of cultural life and entertainment, and now that population density will feel like an ongoing menace rather than a pleasure, I no longer feel like I'm missing something when I'm out of the city. There is nothing to miss!

The pandemic gave me an opportunity to embrace nature. I have even become more intrepid about the cold weather, which I have assiduously avoided until now. I do love nature, but I used to hate the cold. No longer. I've been driven outside by my desire to see my dearest friends and because biking outside offers me a chance to compensate for some of the cardio exercise I've lost due to injury and no gym. Instead of simply tolerating the cold, I've come to embrace the invigorating feeling it gives me and to see that I can indeed, relatively easily, tolerate it. Then there's the staycation I had longed to "take" for many years, but I was too driven to allow myself to stay home. I was always pushing myself out to see the world. The pandemic has granted me the chance to enjoy a staycation. Delicious! Early on, my patient Emma was delighted at the newfound time for introspection and reflection, plus her husband's increased availability.

And then the wheel of life turned, and my patients and I descended into another cycle of negative feelings. The plague dragged on, an open-ended uncertainty. Progress we thought we had made was set back. We regressed.

I just used the word *regress* above in its colloquial sense. But the word is also a term of art in my profession and one that has a great deal of relevance in this moment. Also, I love my work and have noticed that many of my patients appreciate some judicious psycho-ed. Some have even expressed an interest in reading Freud since the pandemic started. So, in that spirit, I will offer the same throughout this book. Regression has always been a useful tool in therapy, an indication of broader changes happening inside the patient—and this is a moment when circumstances are provoking change.

A few quick insights into the knotty concept of regression. Regression is one of those ideas that's easier to understand academically than it is to apply clinically. Simply put, regression is what it sounds like, a process of going backward to an earlier form of behavior and/or felt experience. This can be a good or a bad thing, clinically. If a patient has made a lot of progress and then starts to act out, to get stuck in one of their old dilemmas or problematic behavior patterns, and thus lose the progress they've made, then I worry, of course. At the same time, people often need to go backward in order to go forward. As in, it is always darkest before the dawn. Another metaphor I like to use is this: In order to get to the far bank of the river, one has to traverse cold, muddy water with possible dangerous currents. Any effective therapy includes facing difficult feelings, thoughts, and truths.

In a good analytic process, the patient trusts the therapist enough to allow herself to become somewhat dependent on the therapist, in whatever form dependence takes for that patient. Once the trusting dependence is established, what emerges in analytic sessions are many of the problems, wishes, and fears that occurred earlier in life, particularly in childhood. Regression can also signify states of mind that characterize aspects of childhood stages, such as dependence, passivity, lack of discipline, and rebellion. This is a sign that there is traction between the therapist and patient.

The therapist has more material, including the patient's conflicts around regression, dependence, and so on, to work with, work through, and hope to resolve so that the patient can progress to a more functional mind-set that brings greater life satisfaction. The challenge is that it takes a lot of skill to move through regression to a positive resolution. There is always a danger that a patient either flees, unravels, or gets stuck in an ongoing dependency on the therapist.

While regression is a basic ingredient of therapy, it is not for every patient. Just as butter is a wonderful ingredient, it is not for every meal, can be unhealthy, and may be good to avoid at times.

A related element of my work is cultivating a patient's ability to free-associate. Many people have difficulty free-associating when they first start therapy. A key piece of my work is to encourage a patient's access to free associations. As their facility develops, this indicates that they have found the flow between their conscious and unconscious that enables deep and fruitful work and often improved functioning.

Regression and *free association* are terms that will come up as I talk about my work in this book.

Let's start with a look at what happened in my patients' lives during the pandemic, the intensification of their therapeutic issues, and the new obstacles.

1. Challenges that people had before the virus were accentuated as new and different pressures arose.
2. Coping with loss and grief.
3. Loneliness and isolation.
4. Overcrowding, cabin fever, and new tensions, as the balance was thrown off in relationships between family members and other people living together.
5. Parents with young children were overwhelmed.
6. The separation process for young adults became complicated.
7. Heightened struggles with substance abuse.
8. People did not have their usual solutions and supports.
9. An open-ended timetable exacerbated all these challenges.

Let's dive in.

Challenges That People Had Before the Virus Were Accentuated as New and Different Pressures Arose

Life was simplest in the early days of shelter-in-place when the guidelines were clear and there were few decisions to make. As public venues began to open up (and then close again, and then reopen in reinvented ways), things changed quickly—there was more complexity. Leadership sent mixed messages about what was safe and what wasn't. We were faced with daunting deci-sions, such as how to open schools. Especially difficult were the issues which people were left to make their own decisions about—who with and how to socialize, whether to attend an event or work in person or virtually, and more. Adapting to con-stantly changing circumstances (crises, really) resurfaced and heightened old problems, just as we needed to cope with new ones. This state of flux may bring confusion, anxiety, and even the disappointment of anticlimactic feelings instead of relief.

Susan begins a session by suggesting she cut back and meet only every other week. This idea comes out of the blue from someone well engaged in therapy, dealing with active ongoing challenges in her life and with whom I have a very positive bond. I realize I have to be more proactive with her. Susan takes ref-uge in straightforward and factual way of thinking, and she needs to be pushed in order to free-associate. She insists that nothing is going on. She depends on the external events of her life to give shape to her therapy narrative. This is a retreat to the first phase of her therapy, during which she had difficulty talking freely. She is losing her hard-earned ability to free-associate and direct her thinking inward. After an extended dis-cussion about the concrete events of Susan's life, as limited by the pandemic, I offer that now might be a good time to explore what is going on internally. She takes the prompt. We discuss what's in her head, and then we get into very rich material.

In our next session, she is talking in literal terms a lot again. This time about how France is almost completely reopened and how she is buying groceries these days. I join in her chitchat on those subjects. Then she moves to her hot topic—her marriage and sex as the battleground. My ears are pricked. I listen hyperattentively. After a few forays on my part into deeper waters, I see she can't go there yet. I take a step back into concrete and advisory territory. I recommend setting a schedule for sex with her husband as a way to address both their needs and setting short- and long-term goals for her relationship with him. Then the process starts to flow. Susan wades into deeper psychic waters. We are back to an exploratory and introspective process. I need to be nimbler than in the past.

In our third session after shelter-in-place restrictions began, Ellie wants to change our session length. She wants to shorten it to forty-five minutes from our usual sixty minutes. We begin by discussing the particulars of her work schedule and the physical setting she uses for our meetings. This woman used to be quite resistant to therapy. Much less so now. She likes to challenge me. I know I cannot get into a power struggle with her. She does better when I sidestep the drama of the ubiquitous dominant-submissive structure she imposes in her interactions with people. I agree to a forty-five-minute session, hoping (and inwardly betting) that she will go longer once she settles in to the new normal. She relaxes and brings up an incident with her husband, in which she negated and sabotaged her pleasure with him. This awareness is the fruit of many years of our hard work together. Then, just as we get to the heart of the matter, Ellie ends the session at the forty-five-minute mark. I push her, "This is an example of not allowing yourself to have something, the something being the full sixty minutes to luxuriate in this rich self-discovery in the company of someone (me) who is not leaving you alone with it."

The next session she is late and has difficulty starting, just as she did in the first few years of our work together. I ask what's going on, and she tells me that she's angry I pushed her last session about not allowing her to end the session when she wanted. I agree and apologize. I give her the option of going either forty-five or sixty minutes per session, to be decided by her at the time. This goes a long way with Ellie. At first, she opts for the full sixty minutes. Our next sessions go deeper. She discusses her various forms of self-sabotage. She reacts with near glee when I bring up her tendency toward creating dominant-submissive interactions with others. Then she reverts to a more anxious and tentative state, in which she is more closed to change. I recognize that I've been unintentionally colluding with her by allowing myself to be drawn into conversations that serve Ellie's unintended purpose of avoiding difficult subjects. These conversations can get us off the track. It would be better to point that out, as I often do. I know that now more than ever, she is looking to find herself in my mind as a good person, worthy of love and esteem. She can get to know herself through conversation with me and find herself in my reactions to her. She denies that her recent discomfort in therapy has anything to do with not seeing me in person, though I believe that it does. That will come when she is ready.

A few more sessions later, Ellie brings up her anxiety over life reopening. She has a host of decisions to make about how much to let her medically vulnerable eight-year-old daughter resume activities with friends. I help Ellie grieve the daughter's loss of freedom and the very real limits she has on her life as a result of her rare and severe illness. I help her see that she is also grieving the loss of her dreams of a carefree childhood for her daughter. Rough activities and anything in cold air can trigger serious symptoms. When I hear her start to accept the idea of those limits, I say, "We need limits within which we can find the space to define our choices."

She likes this perspective. It fits with her worldview. After a silence, she tells me that her daughter has gotten interested in online gaming and game design. She has even submitted her first game to a crowdsourcing platform. I say, "Yay." This is what we want for her. My awareness grows. If I am attentive to the subtleties and nuances of the therapy process, surprisingly deep work can be done during the pandemic.

After a stretch of free-flowing narrative, Beth pauses and waits. I mention that she seems to be waiting for something from me. She agrees and wants to know where to go from here. She is in pain because she is facing some difficult truths about herself, her husband, and her beloved sister. We refer to the Mahler baby. A metaphor that has hit the spot for her before.

Margaret Mahler was a psychoanalyst who developed highly regarded theories on infant and toddler development. Although she has not been discredited, her theories do not fit with post-modern ways of thinking. Yet I find some of her theory to be very useful. In early stages of development, as a baby begins to have more locomotion, the ability to crawl and then walk, the baby will always check back with their caregiver. Mahler's theory develops this idea of refueling—that even as a baby crawls away, it derives the comfort and strength to continue exploring by checking back, ensuring it still has a secure home base, gassing up on that safety. Some babies will even crawl back to touch their mother before heading out for another adventure. The parent's role is to provide that home base and say, "It's okay. You can explore some more." Mahler calls this refueling. On the other end of the spectrum, an overly anxious parent may prevent their baby from exploring.

Beth needs me to provide direction and security before she embarks on a new narrative flow. To encourage her further mental adventuring, I offer her some brief psycho-ed about what I learn from seeing where her thoughts go on her own. I know that being alone can feel nihilistic to her and say so. I acknowledge her feelings of being abandoned by her husband and me during the pandemic. In other words, I provide a psychologically secure home base. I see that Beth's classic difficulty, one that has been in abeyance as she has become more secure in our therapeutic relationship (and consequently in life) is making an appearance again in the strange new remoteness.

A few months later, Betsy is angry that the economy is slowly opening up. She has to socialize more. Friends contact her more and want to arrange social get-togethers. Work demands her in-person presence. She was so happy not having to commute to work, to my office, to anywhere. She hates commuting around the city. I agree, silently. How I love not having to commute right now and the freedom of meeting patients on the phone. While I liked video less in the early days of the pandemic (I have come to like it more), I always liked that I can do it from the comfort of my home. More, I can do my work from anywhere. Yay! Freedom to go where I want. I've always envied those people who can work from wherever they want. Now I am one of them. While I miss my patients, I feel physically liberated from the straitjacket of my therapist chair.

At the same time, I sense that Betsy is losing the sense of comfort she derived from coming into my office. The comfort was reaffirmed every time she lay down on my couch, facing me, instead of in the classic Freudian position, facing away from the therapist. She has always needed to see me, to make sure I was still there. She doesn't vocalize these feelings. I read them in the way she has started skipping sessions or calls in late. A vague yet pervasive sense of anxiety and distance inhibit her usual loquaciousness.

As much as I loved my new freedom, I missed being in the physical presence of my patients. I missed them. I missed how much easier it was to practice when I am in their presence, to read their body language and energy, to read the silences. I missed the easy access to patients' cues, without having to concentrate quite so hard.

Betsy won't say she misses me. I think she fears that if she acknowledges her wish to see me, she will have to come to my office, even though she knows I am not ready to return. When I put her separation anxiety into words, she agrees but won't dwell on it. She suffers from an ever-present fear of showing need and desire, especially because, as her therapist, I do not discuss the emotions I feel toward her. She nurses a yearning to lie on my couch with me just feet away from her, like a parent putting a child to bed, at the same time as she dreads having to come back again. I want to tell her that she can feel both simultaneously. But I need to tread delicately. It's hard for her to confront or stay with her longing for me, or for people in general. She can't allow herself to need, miss, or want people. Her early caregivers could not or would not be there for her to satisfy her needs. This makes her wary of relying too much on the presence and ministrations of another. Being solitary is a feeling she is more conscious of and can own up to. She has been delighted with less contact and less socializing. And she's having a host of reactions to missing people, even as she resists the feelings. I can hear her sadness and anxiety when she talks about feeling forgotten, of fearing that she has no friends anymore, when she complains about having to make all the effort with her friends.

We were fortunate to have the lifeline of phone and video during the pandemic, a tool that didn't exist at all, or at least as robustly, before in talk therapy. However, it comes with its losses. At first, I wondered how the new technology would play out over time and how we would adapt to it. Then I realized, I *am* adapting to it. So, the question becomes, what of these accommodations will stick and become hard wired into therapy technique?

Coping with Loss and Grief

We were all dealing with loss at some level during the pandemic. That sense of loss is extending beyond the crisis. We lost a way of life. Even more, we lost a sense of innocence and a uniquely American sense of invulnerability. For an extended period, we lost social and, in many cases, familial contact. This unique crisis deprived a lot of us of the most powerful solace we have to soothe our wounds of loss and hardship—connections with loving and vitalizing others. Alongside the illness itself and depletions of income, this diminution of connection was the most profound loss during the pandemic. Those who used to feel invulnerable have been shaken or completely lost their sense of it. Others, who already understood their vulnerability, have experienced it anew to a sobering and terrifying extent.

Recently, I was shocked to remember people whose company I enjoyed tremendously, like Tilly, whom I saw most Saturdays in my barre class. After class we'd often have breakfast together with two other women I met through her. I loved our frank, spirited conversations, which at times included topics that are normally private and off-limits. From the onset of shelter-in-place, I stopped seeing her. I may never see her again. Cold turkey! There is no replacement for those people and the particular activities and experiences we shared.

The losses are too staggering to calculate right now—we are only really beginning the process of emerging from this crisis. We are recalibrating psychically, after more than a year of trying to protect ourselves from a deadly illness. People lost loved ones to COVID. Some lost the ability to prepare for their death and even to say goodbye. Some lost jobs and income. Almost all of us lost at least some of our social lifelines, the multitudes of personal contacts we so enjoyed throughout the day in the form of colleagues and work meetings, nourishing friendships and a host of transactional human contacts that buoy us throughout our week. Some "lucky" others were quarantined with family members. As we'll see, that "luck" may not have been.

While these losses were mightily hard for adults, they may be even more vital for children of school age and young adults. Social contact contributes to a major aspect of social, emotional, and even intellectual development. We do not know what the long-term effects of losing these all-important building blocks of development are. For babies and children under five, these losses are less deleterious, as long as the nuclear family unit is present. For their parents however, the strain is considerable.

Humans were not meant to raise children without some modicum of a village.

These lifestyle losses were the most profound way in which we therapists were just like our patients during the pandemic. This shared experience allowed us to empathize and sympathize with our patients in the most personal way. This also made it difficult to adequately distance ourselves in the way that we need for analytic reflection. We had to be on guard about that. While we experienced common losses, each of us is uniquely different in our sensibilities. We therapists must take care to stand back and separate ourselves from our patients' dilemmas.

As we know from the statistics, plenty of people experienced the classic loss and grief from the death of a loved one. Frank lost both of his elderly parents to COVID within a very short time frame. Luckily, Frank was one of the exceptions who was allowed to be with his siblings and parents at the time the parents died. His grief was intense, accompanied by a bitter anger over the way the government had mishandled the pandemic, the people who did not take it seriously, and those who endangered others by flouting the rules of social distancing and mask wearing. While this kind of grief is horrible, it is at least recognizable as a grief we understand. For those of us who were "lucky" and did not get ill or lose anyone to COVID, our grief for the loss of social contact and our severely altered lifestyle was harder to recognize and put into words.

In every successful therapy case, the therapist and patient have some significant dynamics in common. This shared experience happened at a whole new level in the pandemic, first because of the degree of it and second because we were going through the experience simultaneously. This profound shift changed the dynamics of authority in the work and had to be newly navigated.

Loneliness and Isolation

Early on, I was surprised to observe that living alone was not necessarily a liability. Among people I knew—family members, friends, and patients—those who were living alone were initially most adept at finding constructive ways to cope and were reporting fewer anxieties than those stuck home with family. Since being widowed, and in spite of missing her husband, my eighty-eight-year-old friend Fern enjoys living alone. Other of my patients who lived alone were relieved and even delighted at having to respond to fewer demands, to have the luxury of time with themselves.

The writer Akwaeke Emezi calls this "witnessing yourself." I love this term because it captures the process of getting acquainted with oneself and also observing oneself at the same time. This is one of the major goals of analytic psychotherapy. My patients who used their isolation to witness themselves tended to be those who had highly developed levels of psychic organization. They reaped some benefits in our new reality.

Can we be a more introspective society as a whole as we emerge from this pandemic? If we can allow ourselves empathy, can we be better equipped to extend empathy more broadly?

These new opportunities for carving out an inner space in which we can be with ourselves led me to deepen my own compassionate friendship with myself, a morsel of personal growth that extends well beyond the immediacy of the pandemic. What do I mean by that? I decided to explore what more I could get out of my own company. How wonderful it was to discover that I enjoyed my own company tremendously. I learned about myself and, through that, about others. I used what I learned to strengthen other important relationships. I plunged into projects that had been put off and that brought me pleasure or made me feel productive or both. I wrote this book. My renewed friendship with myself deepened my understanding of my patients, what they need and how I can help them.

I became intimately acquainted with parts of myself that had peeked through fleetingly in my prior life but never had a chance to fully blossom. Carl Jung called these our shadow parts. We know they're there, but they don't get fully expressed. I realize now, in a way I have not before, that my introverted self is the biggest part of me. Yet introversion doesn't fully define me. I am, for the first time, able to appreciate that I am an extroverted introvert. This realization enabled me to help Nadia.

Newly retired and extroverted, Nadia laments the loss of access to friends and the indoor activities that brought her joy and distraction while she waits for her hardworking husband to retire, which isn't happening anytime soon. We reflected on how to satisfy Nadia's natural extroversion in a period when her ability to recharge with social activities is diminished. I suggested that she may need to get acquainted with the shadow side of herself, the introverted, introspective side, to see what she could get out of that. Most, if not all, people have both sides. It's just that one is more pronounced. Reframing the situation as an opportunity freed her to feel less morose about her loneliness. She was visibly relieved to be released from the hopeless effort of satisfying her hunger for more social contact during the pandemic. This is a moment to take advantage of the opportunity to turn inward. Fighting the circumstances only makes things worse. We must be here now, even if it comes with sorrow and pain. This too shall pass. This is a time to develop compassion for yourself.

That said, as the pandemic settled in for a longer haul (which kept getting longer!), I noticed a marked shift in people's sense of isolation and loneliness, whether or not they lived with others.

Our losses mounted. People were and continue to be in mourning or in need of mourning for these losses. A mourning that can often manifest as anger and despair. People who lived alone were increasingly isolated. People in troubled marriages were stuck together, isolated and lonely, even as they were together. Grandparents wondered when they would see their grandchildren again. For those with substance abuse problems, the challenge was especially pressing. More on that to come.

We do not yet know how we will be affected by these losses in the long term. Based on what I know, observe, and experience in myself and others, I believe that these losses will mature and deepen us as individuals and a nation. We are a young nation and still going through growing pains. Loss is a part of life that we must come to terms with. Some of us will break down. But with the pandemic and its extended impact, we have no choice but to accept and adapt to these unfortunate changes. On occasion, when a patient is facing a harsh moment of reality, I tell them, "Reality is your friend." Even when we get past the acute stages of this pandemic and everyone is vaccinated, this virus will be part of the new normal. Only in accepting this truth can we learn to deal with this reality. Don't fight it. Embrace it and you will thrive. These losses and their accommodations will undoubtedly make us more serious and complete as individuals while nudging us to appreciate more fully the joys and gifts that life does bring. It is no coincidence that we elected a new president, Joe Biden, who embodies the cycle of loss, redemption, maturity, and growth.

Extended periods of loneliness cause physical changes in the brain. Like hunger and thirst, loneliness sends a signal to a person that they need human interaction. The physical effect on our brains can include suppressing our ability to read and remember faces. We can probably all identify ways in which our social abilities and proclivities changed during the pandemic. The good news is that this brain function comes back when we resume human interaction.

In my work, I had to improvise, to provide extra support, to offer a pandemic version of human interaction.

I reach out to Betsy, who I know is having difficulty with me being away for August. She was supposed to reach out to me midmonth. I know she didn't because she is afraid to be needy. She doesn't like that I have the power to withdraw something she needs (me, that is) when she has no say. She dislikes the asymmetry. This pandemic year, for the patients who *need*, as opposed to *want*, my presence in August, I reach out. She is appreciative. I would have done this before, but it feels more pointed this year.

When we speak on the phone, she tells me about her anxieties, feelings of listlessness, hopelessness, and creeping despair. We talk about the effect the pandemic can have on people. I don't say that I am subject to these effects, but it's clear that from our conversation that I am not above the fray. I empathize with her. We are *not* having a session. She is mindful of keeping our conversation short. She asks me how my vacation is in Martha's

Vineyard. I say it's a good vacation as far as it goes in the time of the pandemic, which is more than I would have said before to a patient. I elaborate some about the beauty of nature where I am and how nature is an antidote to the pandemic blues. She tells me about her trip to the Cape and asks me if the Vineyard has a similar atmosphere. She tells me about a dead dolphin she saw on the beach and how she felt about it. I tell her about the man-of-war infestation on Quansoo Beach and the dead horseshoe crabs that I saw earlier in the summer. I repeat the common pandemic phrase "We're all in this alone together." She feels validated and accompanied.

The personal nature, the conversational self-disclosures, and chat were all new and different. This call is just to touch base. We do not get into clinical material. I know that she does not want to feel like a burden. Her fear of being needy would have been aggravated if we had had a *proper* therapeutic session. Betsy simply wants to hear my voice, to feel remembered and to remember me. We psychically touch each other. My willingness to chat humanizes me. Sticking to a rigid format would not have been helpful or mutative. This experience is an example of a way in which practicing therapy during the pandemic moved me toward becoming a warmer and more human therapist.

When Beth becomes unusually anxious during what we had scheduled as a quick check-in during my August vacation, I switch gears on the fly and turn our call into a full session. Unlike with Betsy, the situation called for it.

During a phone session after I'm back, Betsy hesitates, then complains bitterly about her sense of isolation. I make the guess that, in addition to all else, our three-week break during my August vacation has made her connection to me feel more tenuous than usual. As I've mentioned, she has never liked to acknowledge her need for the people she loves and is close to. As a child, she could not count on her caregivers to show up for her, to let her know she was important to them. I comment on her simultaneous tendency to feel forgotten, the need she has for social interaction (which she wants to deny), and her irritation with social demands. I want to tie her current despair to aspects of her background and personal psychology. After our call, I realize that I did her a disservice by not normalizing the depression that was setting in as a result of her social isolation. I feel compelled to do something that is not my norm but which I have done on rare occasions. I call her back and tell her that her feelings are normal and widespread among people today. She feels understood and expresses not only gratitude but relief. My call eases her shame. She understands that she is in good company. Her feelings are a normal human response to isolation and loneliness. My extra outreach opens a door. Now she can be more relaxed, available, and receptive in our work together. As she feels more secure, we can deal with her more difficult emotions.

Susan is unraveling inside and in her body. This is what she does. She always soldiers on. She is a manager, competent and responsible. But her body rebels and tells the story of how she is really feeling. Now her irritable bowel syndrome has flared up and she is experiencing new symptoms from her chronic illness. She is sad and angry and stretched too thin from caring for her elderly father with cognitive decline. Her father has never been nice to her. Finally, at age seventy-five, Susan's father is starting to show some appreciation for his daughter. This pains

Susan. She feels like the love and approval that she has been waiting for her entire life are coming when her father is literally losing his mind and isn't himself. So, in a way, to Susan, it doesn't really count.

Susan longs to be able to turn to her husband for solace and support. Why should this time be any different than other times? He is unable to empathize and show compassion. He continues to press her for love while not giving much in return.

But saddest of all for Susan is that during the pandemic, she can't freely see her grown children and her two grandchildren. This is what she lives for, this and secondarily her large and close group of women friends. On top of it all, Susan and I meet by phone during the pandemic. She drops little hints here and there about how upsetting it is not to see me, but she has too much pride to say it outright. "Am I off getting coffee?" she asks when there's a silence in the session. Then she sends me a long passage from A. A. Milne's *Winnie the Pooh*, all about how deeply, despairingly sad Pooh is, how skeptical he is about ever getting help or of seeing Piglet again. Still, Susan does not opt to meet me on a park bench or a walk for a session. She enjoys the privacy and autonomy of meeting by phone. We humans are complicated creatures and can experience seemingly opposing feelings in the same moment.

I needed to be more active in creating a communication bridge with some patients, between sessions and within the session itself. During the pandemic period, all our contact was attenuated—between me and my patients and, for that matter, between them and the rest of humanity.

Overcrowding, Cabin Fever, and New Tensions, as the Balance Was Thrown Off in Relationships Between Family Members and Other People Living Together

On the other end of the spectrum from isolation (yet very much part of the same continuum), there was overcrowding (even between two people). Ordinary relational tensions were magnified with people squeezed in at home with family members and roommates. All relationships are organized around a certain amount of distance, and each has its own special balance that makes the relationship work well, at best, and be just tolerable, at worst. The pandemic destroyed that balance for its duration. This disequilibrium was especially apparent when grown children returned home and tipped the scales of the parental couple relationship. When children leave home, they leave a vacuum in the family structure as it existed. The deck is reshuffled and parents intuitively need to find a new harmony in their relationship. Sometimes the children were the glue that held the relationship together. Other times, they distracted from the couple's mutually enjoyable intimacy. Usually, it is some combination of both. Grown children returning home throws off the empty-nest balance a couple has found.

Several of my patients and friends noted their irritation with their parents' chewing. Their comments surfaced a memory of my youngest brother complaining to me about my parents' chewing at the dinner table. He was thirteen years old. Soon after he decided to leave for boarding school. At the time, I thought his observation was hilarious, and I understood that it indicated his need to create more space between himself and them. He was living alone with my parents after my other brother and I had left the house. It must have felt painfully quiet at home for him. There I was, years later, with four teen and young adult patients who mentioned this very same irritation during their isolation at home with their parents. We needed some distance to alleviate this collective cabin fever.

There were also the unique tensions of families whose grown children moved back home with them, often temporarily, but nonetheless. Yasu's two grown daughters are at home, one with her boyfriend. Yasu loves being with all of them. He also works a lot and very much enjoys his job. He is a natural intellectual, loves his books and the world of ideas. He is very curious and has a rich internal life. Yet Yasu feels stuck inside and overwhelmed by the monotony and deprivation, the lack of stimulation, the loneliness that can happen, even in the midst of a crowd. As I listen to his cabin fever, I recognize a resonance with the way he reminisces about his paternal grandmother's stories of living in a Japanese internment camp for three years during the Second World War. Yasu's father used to sit under a counter while his mother worked near him in cramped conditions chopping vegetables for community meals. He was bored, starved for company his own age, and felt caged and terribly deprived. The pandemic is not an internment camp, of course, but there are echoes from other trying times.

When Emma's grown daughter comes to live with her for a month, her daughter rearranges all the furniture in the living room, without asking. Emma is furious but also aware of the significance of the unspoken power struggle going on between mother and daughter. She recognizes that her daughter needs to assert her hegemony over her parents. This is a bitter pill to swallow for Emma. She has long savored her role as benevolent matriarch, partly as a way to heal the pain and loss of control she experienced when her own mother died suddenly when she was twelve years old. Emma has become acutely aware of her slipping control as she moves further into her eighties. Her daughter's impositions in the midst of the pandemic were one more reminder.

There were new tensions between some couples and an intensification of tensions for others. For example, when one partner was less strict about social distancing and hygiene. Or there might be discord over the division of domestic labor. A tension that at its root is about feeling devalued by the other, or about equality in the relationship or the lack thereof. Irritating traits in one partner, which used to be tolerable, became unbearable.

Susan's husband continually makes comments and issues directives about how Susan manages and organizes the household. This couple has a traditional domestic arrangement in which her husband works full-time and is the provider and Susan stays home and devotes a prodigious amount of time to homemaking, cooking, and entertaining. These are areas of great skill, joy, and satisfaction for Susan. Her husband's comments stand for ways in which Susan feels controlled, unappreciated, and undervalued for her role in their relationship.

Every marriage is built on a balance between distance and intimacy. The closeness of being with one's spouse 24-7 has yielded some surprising and some not-so-surprising results. I have seen some couples in which the ultra-togetherness has robbed them of a certain privacy that one or both needs. Several of my patients feel unsettled by the goings-on at home with children and other domestic events. These same patients have a very strong sense of privacy and barely feel comfortable meeting virtually for our sessions from their homes. They feel their spouses' eyes and ears are in their therapy sessions. They are itching to get out of their homes and back to their former lives, or at least a life that is more autonomous.

In one couple that I work with, the husband lost his job due to the pandemic. The wife was never employed outside the home. In the past this arrangement worked perfectly well for them. They each appreciated and benefited from not only each other's contributions to the marriage, but each other's personality traits. Now that their implicit agreement about their marital roles has been broken, they no longer see each other with the same golden glow of admiration and harmony. This shift in their marital structure is exposing old aspects of themselves in an unwelcome and novel light. Where harmony was, strife is now raising its head. The shift is requiring much emotional and psychological work and accommodation from both of them.

My marriage was one of those that I thought might not survive my husband working at home. He has a big presence and a resonant and booming voice, which emanates from the central locations in our home, such as our dining room, where he prefers to set up his workstation. I have found that we actually do better with both of us at home. Prior to the pandemic, his office was like quicksand for him. Once there, he could not extricate himself. He would get lost in the work world that resided in his head and forget to let me know when he was coming home, or, if he did, his sense of timing was so off that he might come home two hours after the time he told me. I would be waiting for him in an irritated state of suspended animation, feeling disregarded. We'd often argue when he got home. Now we can see each other working. It's easy to check in with each other. We both like to work a lot and have many interests and projects that take up our individual and separate time so that neither of us is left waiting for the other. We do still argue, sometimes vociferously, and mostly about that old, dreaded chestnut, the division of domestic labor, which falls mostly to me, but we do so less frequently and the times in between are less fraught.

Before the pandemic, my husband and I always had very full independent lives outside of our relationship. Lives filled with lots of work that felt productive and meaningful to each of us, plus hobbies and friendships. We cherished our time together, socializing, taking quiet time just the two of us, and shared activities, like eating out, movies, theater, and, of course and most of all, family! That said, our personalities, sensibilities, and a good deal of our interests are strikingly different. We relied on our independent lives to bear the weight that helped to create our relationship balance. Then we were home together almost 24-7, working, relaxing, and everything else. We adapted quite well (with the exception of the friction around the household chores), as I said above, though less so when our children came home to stay.

Our three sons and their women partners all took turns coming home for a few weeks to a few months at a time. There was a huge silver (even better, gold!) lining in that. We were over the moon when they stayed. At the same time, we had to deal with tensions and accommodations that were difficult and emotionally taxing to navigate within our couple. We paid for our children's presence with some diminishment in our marital harmony. We simply do not get along as well when our children are home for an extended period of time. Divisive mini-alliances pop up. Our attentions are diverted from one another, and the usual household labor that gets unfairly divided falls mostly to me. A whole host of marital issues cascaded out of the overcrowding issues. These tensions forced me to examine the priorities that are most important to me and to let the others fall away or fall down to a lower priority on the list. Occasionally, when I felt I was giving away too much of myself, I asserted a need, knowing that might cause waves. During the pandemic, that need often came down to COVID hygiene. I insisted that all family present in the house wear a mask and suffer the effects of all the first-floor doors kept open when an outsider came into our house. These stringent protections were greeted with a chorus of groans and resistance from my sons, which in turn irritated me greatly. I persevered, or I would have suffered the consequences of my own unbearable anxiety.

There was a continual process of recalibrating, which is in itself part of a larger recalibration of the parent-child relationship as we come to know each other as the real people we are. Not just mother and sons.

These vicissitudes are a particularly sticky result of being thrown together with family members whom we have not lived with for a long time. We see each other in the cold light of day. The distance of time spent away from each other generates new perspectives—parents see more fully who their grown children have become; children see their parents through the non-idealized eyes of an adult. This fresh view, combined with 24-7 living together, plus the hopes and expectations that parents and children bring to one another, unmasked any and all of our collective personal qualities.

In the US, we live in a culture that expects parents to idealize their children, even romanticize them. This is likely truer in upper-middle-class, educated families. Our children are perfect, no matter their less desirable qualities. This idealization accompanies the prevalence of high-anxiety, perfect parenting that has been held up as a benchmark in the last few decades. Parenting is cast as the toughest job around and children as fragile and super sensitive to any "mistakes" a parent makes. When we see vulnerabilities in our children, it can be a hard blow, because we take it personally. We haven't met the standard. We've performed poorly.

This process is accentuated when the adult child has chosen a partner who reflects traits and values important to that child, at least at that time in their lives. Their choice may reflect similarities of one or the other parent, and others may reflect differences. Again, as parents, we may take the implied judgments of these choices personally.

When each of my adult sons were home, the balance of power, alas, shifted in their direction (they may disagree!), while, at the same time, they were confronting my needs as a person, not only as a mother. My assumed and highly prized ability to run my household the way I want was compromised. Despite these adversities, I reminded myself that their presence was worth the sacrifice, at least temporarily. I was lucky to get this unanticipated and fleeting gift of the presence of my children. They are very independent and are all squarely in the middle of launching their separate lives.

Eight months into the pandemic, I met with my peer supervision group of three therapists, all women, to go over cases. Peer supervision is a group that therapists form to review patient cases and get clinical feedback from other peer clinicians. Patients' identities are carefully shielded. In this meeting, in a spontaneous burst of emotion, we became our own cases. We shared revelatory life histories and difficult feelings. No one was judging. Trust was luxuriously high, and everyone could relate or at least respect one another's experiences, quirks, and vulnerabilities. When the two other women asked me how I was, I mean *really* how I was, I said, "If I answer, I can only answer the unvarnished truth." Body postures visibly relaxed. Facial expressions lit up. They said, "Bring it on. We need it!"

We told stories of living with our adult children (and grandchildren, in some cases) either in our home or in our children's. We shared joys, surprises, mysteries, and hurt feelings (on both sides). We poured out our feelings and then sat back and explored and analyzed the dynamics between ourselves and our beloved children. The authentic heartache of true love accompanied our unexpected conversation.

We mourned the asymmetry of our relationships with our children. They are still the most important people in the world to us, even as we no longer have that same priority for them (well, maybe somewhere buried deep down, but who cares about that!). We acknowledged and named this latest, unprecedented iteration of their separation. Living with our grown children had accentuated this new and painful process.

This is in the nature of psychological separation. As children who have returned to the nest, we learn who they truly are. We can no longer hang on to any illusions we may have had. They learn the same about us. The reality comes as a shock to both parties. We realized that some of what we saw was probably a product of regression to some revised, uncomfortable parent-child dynamic. The choreography of this dance was neither smooth nor lyrical, charged with passion and emotion.

Together, we three therapists examined the different dynamics in our own lives from every angle—sons and mother, daughters and mother, our children's children, fathers, of course, plus our children's romantic partners. We examined the effects of our socioeconomic status. All our children were brought up with plenty, more than we were. We empathized with our children and the pressures they are under, and we grieved for ourselves and the way we were being forced to divest some of our huge investments in their well-being. We laughed at the ways our children treated us as silly and dumb, with our PhDs, extensive postdoctoral educations, and careers based on thinking deeply.

We commiserated about how closely we are knit together with our children, but also how separate we are from them. How sad and wonderful it is for us that they lead their own lives and follow their own hearts and values. How the privilege, both internal and external resources, they were raised with complicates their separation. Why their fathers, our husbands, often are spared their harsh recriminations. How they are a part of us, and how we have to let them go, in a way that we had not imagined. How we wanted to be perfect mothers, but are not. How our children, once perfect in our eyes, are not perfect, but still beloved and, best of all, real people.

The pandemic offered us an opportunity to learn about family members and our relationships with them. Yes, we've had plenty of rough patches in this petri dish of different generations of family moving back in together. In our family, we have used these tensions to get to know one another in a real way. We better relate to each other based on who we really are (always a work in progress), as opposed to what we wish each other to be. We get along better. We get to choose how to see our relationship evolution, the spin we will put on the experience. If we can accept each other as individuals (not clay people to mold to our liking), we have something to gain.

This flow of losses, tensions, and petty degradations has increased my humility and my ability to appreciate and not judge my patients' distress over their experiences of shifting family dynamics, with their joys, sorrows, power structures, losses, and compromises.

Parents With Young Children Were Overwhelmed

Parents, mothers, and especially working mothers of young children, were overwhelmed, resentful, and sad. Finding relief in the form of paid help was not necessarily safe and, at minimum, it was stressful to figure out how to work that out. Parents (again, mostly mothers) were called upon to become their child's teachers and IT specialists. These are generally roles that parents never bargained or trained for. They are also roles that demand almost full-time attention, taking away from the parents' jobs, housework, and downtime.

These overwhelmed parents were utterly exhausted. Some were angry at feeling like they've lost their very selves, that they gave over way more than they ever felt possible or wanted to the care of their children. That they were neglecting themselves. These aggravations naturally spill over into their partner relationships, especially when one partner was taking on the lion's share. It was like asking someone at work to take on another employee's full-time job while continuing with their own demanding job, never mind having a personal life. Some parents felt like they were about to break.

Nancy has four elementary school–age children born within six years of one another. The youngest two cannot manage the technical aspects of their online learning on their own. Nancy is on call to help them during the school day. At the end of the school day, Nancy reports that her children need her to structure the rest of their day. Nancy let her housekeeper go because she did not feel safe having her commute during the pandemic. Not only does Nancy have her own full-time business, but she does not yet have an assistant for this fledgling business, which has taken off much faster than she expected when she started it only a couple years ago. She loves her business and regrets having to shift her focus away from her efforts to build and solidify her sense of self and confidence through her business. She is a perfectionist, who insists on keeping a spotless house and also worries about maintaining a loving connection with her husband, who is also tired from working hard at his job. Nancy feels like all the plates she is juggling are about to come crashing down around her.

For many women, the plates have already come crashing down. Nancy and others like her have borne the brunt of pandemic related job losses and damaged careers as they have felt forced to quit their jobs or at least withdraw their energies from their work because of increased childcare duty. Many feel that these shifts have caused a major setback in the gains women have made in the job market and their overall status in society.

Parents are not only overwhelmed, they are also worried about the impact of the pandemic on their children. The effect of no school, virtual school, and of limits on their social interactions are indeed a worry. Yet plagues are a feature of life on this earth. No one is born with a guarantee that they are entitled to escape any or all plagues. We must learn to accept, incorporate, and adapt to what the pandemic is doing to us. Our children will be affected. They will be pandemic children in all their uniqueness. They will contribute to the world out of their particular experiences of having lived through this era. It is the job of their adults to help them live with the pandemic, not in denial of it, and to figure out how to adapt, compensate for, and work with their circumstances. I suspect that over time we will see that those pandemic children who adapted, whose adults supported them wisely and non-critically, will have something unique to offer to the world.

Pam runs a close-knit family with a great sense of purpose, and run it she does. Yet she does so with a light and loving touch. Pam empathizes with the hardships her sons are experiencing during the pandemic, missing their friends, putting up with the frustrations of Zoom schooling and the rigors involved in following COVID safety protocols. Pam meets her sons halfway by arranging outdoor playdates and other safe social gatherings. She helps them buy the clothes they need and regulates their social media connections so that their wishes are balanced against the limits that Pam and her husband impose on their screen time. Their family life is rich with connection, communication, and shared, meaningful activities, including a significant religious life. Pam and her husband carve out a space for their sons to be heard. They plan fun outings and join their many religious holidays with family, food, and hanging out. The children are thriving, doing well in school, and developing their own distinct personalities and interests.

That said, now, in the twelfth month of the pandemic, many other young schoolchildren and their families are in crisis. Virtual school is not working as a steady diet. It may have worked as a stopgap measure, but few children can sustain their attention and engagement to school through a computer screen. So children are not being educated, they are entertaining themselves online to a much greater degree than ever before, and they are irritable and lonely for their peers. Parents are not equipped to fill the gap, and parents who need to work are at a special disadvantage. Some families are getting exposed to COVID because their children simply cannot go without any social interactions at all and they feel like they have no choice but to put themselves and their families at risk. The only solution is to make school accommodations a priority. I do not purport to be an expert on what that would look like. Whether it is vaccinations for all teachers and school staff, sophisticated air-purifying systems, clear and enforced COVID protocol with masking, social distancing, etc., it must be done.

The Separation Process for Young Adults Became Complicated

Adolescents and young adults confined with their families experienced an acute and particular type of loneliness and isolation. I do a lot of work with adolescents and young adults. I was particularly struck by the pathos of their predicaments during the pandemic.

The loss of their peers had a deep impact. The conditions of sheltering with parents were unnatural for adolescents and young adults, in least in our American culture. Psychically, they are working on separating. But the pandemic interfered with the natural separation process of adolescents and young adults, in some cases delaying separation and, in others, throwing gasoline on a sensitive process. Many were cast back into their parents' homes, just as they were progressing through the fraught and attenuated process of splitting off from the feathered parental nest. They were making forays into the bewildering launch of their adult lives, finding their sea legs. Then they were consigned to their parents' homes. Some were young, working adults. Others were high school and college kids who hadn't yet moved out or who lived at home during school breaks. Some were happy to have the option of moving back, and some went reluctantly. Love, work, relationships, and privacy all had to be negotiated anew as families navigated their pandemic togetherness.

Kevin just turned twenty-four. He is very close with his parents. And he is working on figuring out who he is distinct from his parents. This important psychological separation is my therapeutic goal for him. Kevin's aims are more literal. He wants to discuss everyday conflicts and dilemmas—how he feels about his recently ex-girlfriend, whom he does and does not want to continue to be friends with, what activities he wants to do with her, and so forth. There is a difference between what the patient is working on manifestly and how the therapist hears it. When all goes well, as a patient progresses in therapy, those separate goals become more closely aligned in the patient's consciousness.

Kevin and I worked together from when he was twelve years old to eighteen. We resumed working together two years ago, when he was twenty-two. In this second phase of our work, Kevin continues to work primarily on his inhibitions and insecurities around socializing, his indecision about breaking up with his girlfriend of five years, the breakup itself (which happened about a year prior to the pandemic), and the bitterness and regret that surfaced after the breakup. He feels that he allowed his ex-girlfriend to undervalue him in the last year of their relationship. The severity of the breakup was like a divorce in Kevin's young life. It requires him to reassess who he is as a person, his likes, desires, dislikes, and values. It even calls into question various aspects of Kevin's relationship with his parents, as is always the case when a young person chooses a partner, even one they may not marry. Increasingly, when Kevin discusses these topics, his narrative drifts to friction he feels with his parents. They say they miss his girlfriend. They say that he is to blame for his own unhappiness in the relationship. They push him to reach out to her.

But Kevin has realized, through our work, that he is more of an introvert than he had thought. He is happy in his own company for extended stretches of time. He is content with a relatively quiet social life and a few friends he truly cares about. This makes his parents anxious. They continually exhort him to nurture his friendships, check in with friends he hasn't spoken to recently, make dates with friends, invite them over, and so on. Because Kevin looks up to his parents and has always depended upon them, their admonishments about keeping up an active social life undermine his confidence in his own knowledge of himself. As we work together, Kevin is taking tentative steps toward strengthening his resolve to follow his instincts. Yet his parents' presence looms large in his mind and often threatens to override his intentions.

While separation happens internally and is less about whether a young adult is living with their parents or not, living at home complicates the process of becoming an independent and separate individual. Kevin's situation is further complicated because there is so much love between his parents and him. But it is a love that masks other mixed feelings, including Kevin's anger and resentment at feeling controlled and not accepted for who he is. The nature of their love does not make separateness easy. His parents demand closeness and togetherness, which can't be forced and may not be the most beneficial condition for Kevin at this time in his life. For example, Kevin's parents often treat him as an auxiliary parent to his sister, who is ten years younger.

Prior to the pandemic, Kevin spent all his vacation and break time from college at home. When the pandemic hit, he moved home from the apartment where he'd been living. Kevin's struggle to make sense of his relationship with his ex continues in full swing. The relationship issues he is struggling with have been brought into sharp relief by the circumstances of living at home. Kevin is pushing uphill to find his own way to choose his friends (including girlfriends) and conduct his friendships, in other words, to be himself. Because of his close bond with his parents, coupled with his own insecurities, Kevin finds it difficult to resist their entreaties and follow his own heart. Living at home is complicating his separation mightily.

In a normal separation process (to be precise, what we, Americans, have thought of as normal until now), where the grown child is living independently, they may do things that the parent disapproves of. This is an important part of the process, which cannot occur without friction when family members are living together.

At twenty-eight years old, Elizabeth left her apartment in New York City when the pandemic started. She moved to Florida to live with her mother and brothers. She was able to work from home. Her new boyfriend joined her. When Elizabeth first started therapy with me five years ago, she often did not know how she felt and what she wanted. Elizabeth was more comfortable reflecting someone else's desires. Her pattern was to cater to the other person, her boyfriend at the time, or her mother or brother, until her submission started to chafe. Until the year prior to the pandemic, she often volunteered for work projects in faraway locations to further her career. The trips were also a way to escape her previous boyfriend. She wanted to break up with him but couldn't because he didn't want the relationship to end, and her default was to submit. On her trips, she often spent hours on the phone with him. He would latch onto her, refusing to let her go. Her mother forbade her to bring this boyfriend home when she visited. Eventually, after protracted and painful work together, supported by the loosening effect of the trips, Elizabeth ended that relationship.

So by the time the pandemic starts, Elizabeth is on a solid path to finding herself. She has a new boyfriend who stirs feelings in her, allowing her to make contact with her inner emotional life in a way she has not been able to since before her father died. Naturally, her feelings for the two men are different in kind, but her reactions to her boyfriend have evoked Elizabeth's capacity for deep love and attachment and vulnerability that she has kept sealed away for many years now. These feelings have in turn opened a path toward a passion, caring, and genuine ness that I never doubted was present but that has been buried for a long time. She has identified a new career that satisfies her more and is on course to begin a prestigious training program in that field. She is starting to question her mother's dominance and influence over her and to separate out her feelings and wishes from those of her mother.

Then Elizabeth moves into a rental house, just down the street from her mother's house. At first, the conflicts with her mother present themselves in minor daily irritations. Her mother pops by every day, often uninvited, plopping herself down for a chat, making suggestions about whom Elizabeth should see and what she should do. Then Elizabeth's mother tells her that it is imperative that she resume her old family role of including her differently abled younger brother in all her activities and outings with her friends and boyfriend. When Elizabeth plans a trip to visit her boyfriend's family in a different state, her mother tells Elizabeth to use the family car instead of her own. She proposes Elizabeth take a different route from the one Elizabeth and her boyfriend have plotted out. She asks Elizabeth to call her every day. She shares her unsolicited concerns about the safety of the route, their departure time, and the length of the trip. Elizabeth's hard-won confidence is faltering under the challenge of her mother's constant presence.

Starting in adolescence or even before, kids naturally want to spread their wings and move toward autonomy and away from dependence. This momentum builds throughout childhood and really gets gassed up during adolescence, taking to the air in late adolescence. Late adolescence as a developmental stage of life can reach well into one's twenties.

With pride and joy, Larry reports that when his parents were away recently for a week, he got up early, made a structured schedule, achieved some goals, and took care of the house. This previously independent young man has been home from law school for just under a year, after his MS worsened. He has been forced to rely heavily on his parents' care both because he has been so ill and because of the pandemic. His illness puts him at greater risk for the pandemic. He has been more homebound and dependent than he could have imagined. Over the past few months, I have worked with Larry and his family to pry parents and son apart so that Larry can progressively take over his self-care and responsibilities while he recovers from his illness. He tells me he soared while his parents were away. We agree that he relinquished his independence when he came home ill, because he needed to recuperate. Like riding a bike with training wheels, he used his parents' care to rebuild his internal strength. By the time his parents went away, he was able to ride on his own, to put his newly regained strength into action. The regression he has experienced in his year of dependence during the pandemic caused unavoidable friction between him and his parents. Yet, in the end, he uses his enforced, painful, and unwanted dependence to grow.

Listening to my "separating" patients during the pandemic, I wondered whether I needed to reconceptualize my views on what is typical in this process and what kinds of environments are optimal for psychological separation and development. In the US, we have always valued distance, independence, and autonomy. We used to be one of the few countries that expects our children to leave home for college at age eighteen, only returning home for holidays, and then to complete that process at age twenty-two, when they graduate from college and move out on their own. Now the experience of teens and young adults moving home looks much more similar to many other cultures around the world who view (or used to view) this kind of dependence more warmly or at least benignly. I imagine that those cultures work through the separation process differently and with a different lens than we do in our culture. Is it time to adjust my lens as I listen to my patients? Time will tell. I will watch and listen to these dynamics attentively.

Heightened Struggles With Substance Abuse

For those whose sense of self is shaky and for whom the isolation is overwhelming, the inability to avoid their inner life without their usual supports can threaten any stable base they may have built. Some of my patients returned to addictive substances in an effort to shore up their defenses. These are patients who simply have to work that much harder to stave off depression and anxiety. Their resilience is not as robust as other people's, and outlets, such as nature, do not offer them enough solace.

Embedded in a broader discussion of his intense feelings of panic and his weed usage, Frank mentions that he has cut down to two (pipe) bowls of weed a night. He offers the information without a comparative reference to how much he had been smoking prior to cutting back. The information conveys a lot about how much he was smoking. Over the past months, Frank has become increasingly distraught over the deaths of his parents from COVID complications. In a roundabout way, to demonstrate that I understand the magnitude of the pain that he is in, I remind him of the power of weed to numb feelings. Before I leave for the month of my August vacation, Frank tells me that he is doing so well that he might cut back on his therapy. While I am away, I consider whether cutting back is a response to a healthy wish or a reaction to my going away at a difficult time. I think about whether his statement is, in part, a reaction to some way in which I may have had trouble absorbing the enormity of his pain, or whether he holds back on expressing the depth of his pain under most circumstances. As so often happens in treatment, my hunch is that we collude with one another in hiding something that we could not fully contemplate on the eve of my vacation. When I am back, we take up the challenge together. His comment about cutting back on smoking clarifies how hard this period is for him. I have not fully appreciated the extent and depth of his anguish. His grief is heightened by the nightmarish political situation, which is the literal reification of his frequent apocalyptic nightmares. He does not cut back on therapy. Our work together continues thoughtfully and not reactively.

People Did Not Have Their Usual Solutions and Supports

In these conditions of extraordinary adversity, we all had fewer resources available to shore up our ability to cope with the extra challenges and life in general. A common thread among all my patients, those who live alone and those who were thrown together, was that they, and I, were missing our usual solutions and supports. People who lived alone had pre-pandemic lives full of social, work, and leisure activities that provided the structure, company, and purposefulness that they needed. Those who lived with others had developed outlets and separate lives as well as ways of carving out their own space in a way that they achieved the balance of closeness and distance that they needed. All that changed. The rug was pulled out from under us. We lost what kept us regulated, sane, and happy. We lost our sense of purpose, structure, and routine. Our true supports supplement our coping skills in positive ways (as opposed to distractions, which create the appearance of coping, by papering over our internal struggles with busyness). While people with jobs may have been less bored and anxious because they felt more of an ongoing sense of purpose, even with our work to keep us occupied, we needed more support. I was fascinated by the fact that there were no generalizations about who suffered more, those living alone or those squeezed together with family members.

There's more silence and recalcitrance than usual in the beginning of Hannah's session. Entombed within the silence are Hannah's implicit and recent negative feelings toward me and therapy, triggered by the present but fueled by ancient feelings transferred from painful childhood experiences. These feelings are embedded within the overall positive emotional tone of our relationship. Hannah makes inferences about feeling like giving up. This is her proverbial death instinct speaking. To understand why these feelings are coming up now, I put what I'm hearing in this session together with what I already know about Hannah from our many prior sessions. I have a hunch that the combination of her pregnancy and the loss of routines and social contact as a result of the pandemic make her feel terrified, small, and cut adrift. My experience tells me that she feels abandoned, like when she was a little girl and felt entombed at home with her parents. I decide that I have to speak more and save her from herself. My silence and physical absence, because we are, of course, meeting virtually, is like the empty home where she grew up. Her parents were there, but not there, as if estranged. They left her (the baby of the family) so that they could party.

Rage comes up first for Hannah, but behind that is her fear. She is afraid of the potential destructiveness of her own rage. She cannot reflect on her feelings, the way she usually can, without more intervention from me. I feel I am losing her. I talk, hoping that my flow of words will trigger some helpful clarity and insight. I am making it up as I go along. I interpret vigorously without the usual amount of material from Hannah. I know her well and I count on that to make meaningful interpretations. As I am speaking, the links that connect my understanding float up from my own pre-consciousness. In a barely audible, little girl voice, she thanks me for filling the silence.

In the next session, I take heart from the trusting re-alliance. I confront her about my concerns—the disordered eating, her intense anxiety, depression, and withdrawal and even more, shame. Internally, I worry about whether she will resist the temptation to return to the weed that was such a comfort to her before her pregnancy. She has valiantly avoided any substances since conception. Finally, we get to the effects that her behavior will have on the fetus. We delve in to her painful and bitter fears for the fetus and what harm she might be doing. Then we reach her deepest shame—her ambivalence about this highly desired pregnancy.

I've already mentioned Susan, who used to rely on her hands-on involvement with her children and grandchildren and how useful and loved she felt by them. She also got support in the camaraderie and validation from her large and close circle of friends, with whom she got together with frequency pre-pandemic. Emma missed the active role she played prior to the pandemic in ferrying her grandchildren to school and their activities and in general being available to be called upon to spend time with them when that was needed. Betsy relied on the routines of her work, the art classes that gave her weeks color, and the select, cherished friends she spent time with going to concerts, walking, and casually hanging out. All these supports were gone during the pandemic.

The news was not all bleak. There were some new or redis-covered sources of support, which I've mentioned already and will get to in more detail in a moment.

A number of my patients appreciated that they had the time and space to get in touch with their inner life and feelings, to witness themselves, as I mentioned earlier. I, too, was delighted by the decreased need to respond to social requests, as much as I loved my pre-pandemic social life.

Several of my patients mentioned the soothing effect of nature as another touchpoint for solace—an effect I have felt, too. In her book *The Well-Gardened Mind*, the psychiatrist and psychotherapist Sue Stuart-Smith writes that, particularly when people are facing illness and end-of-life crises, they find in nature, especially gardens, a sense not only of life, but of the renewal of life. Finding joy in new life is a widespread and natu-ral mood enhancer, like the joy that grandparents experience with grandchildren. The pandemic posed an existential threat. Being outside, especially in nature or a garden, was a substitute for pre-pandemic social engagements, entertainment, and just plain being out and about in the world. While some people enjoy nature and being outside more than others, we all need nature and the outside world. The green, the sunlight, and the Vitamin D all satisfy a biological need and help us to keep our moods elevated and offer us support and relief when our usual solutions are unavailable. Our renewed appreciation of nature will hopefully boost our support of President Biden's environmental and climate agenda. Still, nature is not everyone's solution, nor a complete answer. The struggle to find substitutes for our usual support structures is ongoing.

An Open-Ended Timetable Exacerbated All These Challenges

When the pandemic started, most people assumed that the crisis would be a relatively short-lived phenomenon. Then when it became clear that there was no early expiration date, the open-ended nature of the situation exacerbated people's fears and feelings of helplessness. For people who are especially troubled and less sturdy, this can feel like annihilation anxiety, stress that their world as they know it will disappear and that they will disappear or be destroyed with it.

Victor E. Frankel writes about how difficult it was for the prisoners in Auschwitz to reconcile not knowing how long they would be confined. Quoting an unnamed psychologist, he describes this condition as "a provisional existence of unknown limit." While it would be wildly inappropriate to compare the circumstances of the pandemic to life in a German concentration camp, the concept that the open-ended nature of crisis conditions makes it that much harder to manage psychologically is well established. Frankel stresses that the only redemptive way to cope is to find a sense of inner meaning and conviction, which can confer an inner freedom. I, too, believe that, apart from the all-important practical tools for coping, such as structure, routine, and pleasurable and/or purposeful activities, the single most important tool for coping and getting through the pandemic with any kind of resilience was to find meaning in how one structures and thinks about one's everyday life. For me it was and continues to be work, writing, domestic projects, and family. The privilege of helping patients as well as writing this book and all that it entailed, such as making observations, taking notes, and thinking about the effects of the pandemic on people, gave me a sense of meaning, even as I was living through the pandemic. Recording what I learned is one of the things that makes me feel that this confining and scary experience had a purpose.

Finn reports a dream in which no one he loves and depends on is available to him. As we explore the dream, we realize that his feelings of isolation and despair have been triggered by multiple circumstances, all exacerbated by the current conditions under the pandemic. His wife is consistently in an unusually bad mood, the result of worrying that her recent abdominal surgery has not been a success. He is also dealing with temporary dizziness, caused by a recent illness (not COVID) that required hospitalization. And I am just back after a three-week absence for my annual August vacation. The accumulation of absences psychologically plunges him back into the ways in which his parents could not feed his emotional thirst for understanding and meaning. But, of course, the larger backdrop is the pandemic. The pandemic has restricted his access to the deep comfort of being with the people he loves. Interacting with people soothes him, distracts him and gives him buoyancy. Finn is in his sixties. In addition to his recent illness, he has a chronic illness that makes him more susceptible to COVID. So he must be even more careful than the average person. As the pandemic drags on, he feels like he has served his sentence. With no clear end in sight, he cannot buoy his mood. He feels isolated, lonely, and estranged, like when he was a child, dependent on parents and older siblings who couldn't understand. The pandemic, the illness of our government systems, and his own recent illness trigger Finn's memories of the terrifying early days of his diagnosis and chronic illness, compounded by the forbidden nature of the subject of illness in his family of origin. The pandemic circumstances have resurfaced his past trauma.

I experienced this same open-ended uncertainty alongside my patients. I had to figure out how to be both partner and guide to them. I could not pretend that I knew more in the strange new world we shared. Yet I owed them the calm and confidence needed to do my work as a therapist. I mostly achieved that balance, with room for mistakes. The mistakes are always part of the process. If I get too hard on myself about getting it wrong on rare occasions or trying something new that feels daring, I will become paralyzed. That did not happen. Quite the reverse—I became energized. I was and continue to be the evenly balanced, observant scientist, mentally recording the data, as well as the artist, trusting in my training, experience, and intuition. My trust in myself is being tested. The boundaries and practices of therapy shifted and continue to shift.

CHAPTER THREE

Refreshed Approaches to Therapy (and My Own Personal Evolution)

In any period of destabilization, there is an opportunity for renewal and reinvention. I am a developmentalist. Developmentalists understand that right before a child (and, I would add, adults as well) enters a new stage of development, they often go through a period of psychic reorganization that looks like regression. This understanding offers a possible way in which patients' regressions during the period of the pandemic opened up a chance for deeper, productive work. I urged patients to connect more with their inner life, to take advantage of less going on externally.

At the same time, I felt a personal opportunity opening to reinvent my practice. I love to make things up myself, to be creative. This was my chance. For example, as I shifted my approach to self-disclosures, I sensed the opportunity to touch on new and different aspects of my patients' psychic experience.

I had an opportunity to sharpen my listening and observational skills.

I also found renewal in the fresh opportunity I had to move more. During the early days of the pandemic, I sometimes walked during phone sessions. I sensed that the movement made me more active in the work of therapy. I observed how movement affected my interventions and interpretations and how my walking felt for the patient. I told them when I walk. Because I was at home, I could transition between patient sessions and housework, so I stayed in motion that way, too, and felt freer.

I am incorporating more meditation and mindfulness-style approaches to my work, too, plus some ideas from Somatic Experiencing, bringing a focus to what is going on in the patient's soma, their body. In some cases, I recognize that there is nothing required but to be present with the patient. *Nothing* can be the hardest response for a therapist—we feel useless. But more often than before, all that a patient might need is for me to witness, with my presence, their real-life problem, their loneliness or sadness, that they are stuck at home in an unhappy marriage, that they have lost some or all of their income or lost a parent to COVID and couldn't say goodbye in person. Part of my role as therapist is to psychically hold difficult emotions for the patient when they cannot yet bear the full brunt on their own. Larry had to take an open-ended leave of absence from law school. Then he suffered a debilitating setback in his MS, which caused him to move back in with his parents. He had many losses to grieve. I grieve with him. Contributing *nothing* can be more difficult to achieve than active interventions or interpretations.

I believe that incorporating my own *self* into my work is essential now: integrating my intuition. Allowing myself to draw on my unique subjectivity and sensibilities, my upbringing, my values and experiences. Incorporating the influences that come from outside my psychoanalytic training more intentionally, not to impose my opinions, to influence or to lecture, but rather to inform my thinking as a part of my tool kit.

Some of my influences: I have a lot of lawyers in my life—my husband, my best friend, my father, my eldest son. I have always appreciated the legal model of delving for the truth. Law combines the same analytic rigor as psychoanalysis, while also benefiting from the craft and artistry of the lawyer. In my work, I will often ask a question to which I think I know the answer. I ask it knowing that the answer is important to bring to light in words, and more importantly, it will enable my patient to discover something about themselves for themselves.

In that same vein, my background in ballet has influenced my facility with combining rigor and artfulness. Ballet combined joy and freedom with strength and solidity. I had the freedom to express how I felt inside—extending my body to its ultimate limit, a soaring reach for the horizon, making sculpture in motion. Ballet offered harmony and safety. There was the predictable and reassuring structure of the ballet class—barre first, center of the floor second, and across the floor last. At the barre there was a set order. We always started with pliés, then tendues, frappés, and other movements, working up to rondes de jambe, grand battements, and so on. In the center, there was a similar order of dance variations like adagio, culminating in the big jumps and turns across the floor. There was

lavish variety and room for artistry, within the reassuring predictability of the structure and order of things. There was the
diversity of different teachers' varied use of the same techniques.
I acquired a rich body language that allowed me to express
myself through the physicality of ballet. And always, there was
beauty, the mess of life cleaned up.

To be sure, I was disciplined before ballet. In dance, I found
a métier through which to express my discipline. Psychoanalytic therapy makes the same demands of its practitioners. The
therapist balances her intuition (her artistry) with the discipline
of her intellect, then draws on her very personal self to round
out the harmony of her work.

Ballet was also a practice ground for stretching myself to the
maximum, for cultivating a deep expertise, for always returning to the physical core of the body, just as therapists always
return to the patient's experience as the core of the work. We
cannot over-rely on theory or our own subjectivity. We must
balance—that beautiful word and practice. Balance. Is that part
of my attraction to therapy? I always loved the balances in ballet. In therapy, we are always finding the balance between the
various sources we draw upon for practice—theory, our "third
ear," reality, the unconscious, how the patient brings her subjective experience into her behavior toward the therapist, and
the meaning of the therapist's personal reactions toward the
patient. We are always refining, retooling, and tweaking the
balance of intuition versus intellect.

From my very first ballet class, I felt like I got it. As the great
Russian dancer Nijinsky said, "You just feel it." From my very
first ballet class, I understood how the movement was supposed
to feel in my body. In tendues, one of the basic building block

movements, I knew instinctively to slide my foot against the floor as I extended it as far as it would go, gently and gradually lifting my heel off the floor, then my instep until my foot finally formed into a pointed arch with just my toes touching the floor, a movement fit for the French king who invented it. The impatient teacher would demonstrate the wrong way to do it for the rest of the class—"You don't just put it out there. You present. You must slide it out, hugging the floor until you release." But I already knew what to do instinctively. I felt so at home in my body, so at harmony with who I was, instinctive and intuitive. That's how I feel working with patients while practicing therapy.

I came upon another resonant influence recently while reading Admiral William H. McRaven's book *Make Your Bed*. While his pull-yourself-up-by-your-bootstraps approach is not the way to do therapy, his line of thinking helped me sort out my own thoughts on finding the balance of empathy that's appropriate to offer in my practice. Empathy and the ability to take the patient's perspective is essential in the practice of therapy. However, too much empathy can stall a patient's development. McRaven's book reminded me to listen for when a patient is so weighted down by feeling badly that they can't get on with life and don't have the ability to say to themselves, "Just do it." Sometimes feeling and insight and confidence follow when there is no other choice but to act.

McRaven's book made me realize that I had given my sons too much empathy while I was raising them. This was my way to compensate for the empathy I had craved while growing up. Now I live with that pain and the challenge of empathizing with myself and my own parental shortfall.

Beth's husband is stressed in his new job and blames her for not being supportive enough, taking his anxiety out on her. It hasn't occurred to her to say, "What about me?" Her instinct is to wonder how she can help him get out of his stress, so that she, in turn, can be out of the line of fire. I say, thinking about McRaven, "You may never naturally put yourself first. You may have to remind yourself to put yourself first. That may have to be a deliberate thing."

Earlier in my career, drawing on my own *self*, my intuition, and my personal theories would have provoked much more anxiety than it does now. That is the nature of doing something different, new and creative. The combination of my long clinical experience, not to mention life experience, and the exigencies of the pandemic stripped away another important layer of anxiety.

The pandemic catalyzed a process of reinventing how therapy is done. I find this exciting but also fraught with uncertainty. In my mind, I hear a chorus of colleagues responding that I am being wild, irresponsible, and unwise. As you'll read, I am in no way suggesting that we throw out the baby with the bathwater. I am not advocating for exploring uncharted territory. Rather, I think we need to base our reinventions on the bedrock of theories that are already long established in our field. At the same time, we need to free ourselves from the shackles that bind us to conditions that no longer exist, or are temporarily missing, as well as traditions that are no longer effective. It is extremely challenging to hold a tension between the two. We are on our own in unprecedented times. Can we dare to color outside the lines?

One of my inspirations for change in the work of therapy comes from fashion designers' responses to the pandemic. While I am not a fashionista, I do enjoy it and have always followed it. I associate fashion with warm and pleasant memories, a loving bond I had with my mother. She would call me in when she got her monthly *Vogue* magazine, and we would lie on her bed and flip through the glossy magazine together. Lovingly and admiringly, she would point out which styles would look good on me and make commentaries on her opinions of certain designers, their looks, and the nature of their artistry. When I got old enough to be able to wear real fashion, she would source pretty pieces for me from various sales and reduced-price providers and enjoy watching me wear them. My mother's main way of showing her love for me was through her appreciation of the way I looked.

I have subscribed to *Vogue* for my entire adult life. As much of fashion photography has devolved into wacky and outrageous displays, with a de-emphasis on classic beauty, I have become less interested in *Vogue*. Yet I am unable to relinquish my subscription. I would feel incomplete without the broad outline of what the look is each season.

With the advent of the pandemic, I was curious to see what was going to happen to fashion and how *Vogue* magazine was going to cover it. Designers and fashion pundits have all said that the pandemic was or should be bringing about a revolution in fashion. Just as the internet and phone for therapy were growing in popularity prior to the pandemic, and then burst out as the only way to meet during the pandemic, fashion had also been progressively changing direction.

Most designers had begun already to consider sustainability or upcycled swatches of fabric, use of local products and styles, aka community fashion. More, they were starting to put a political lens on fashion. These trends have been evolving for years now.

Then, with the pandemic, Tory Burch and Joseph Altuzarra were speaking out about making less of everything. Balmain's Olivier Rousteing and Pierpaolo Piccioli of Valentino talked about presenting fashion in different settings, such as online, instead of the big fashion shows. Models may show designers' clothing in the places where the models live and spend time. Luxury and couture will give way to necessity. Clothing may not be sold seasons ahead of the time, but rather when people want to wear the clothes, during the season that matches the clothing. Couture clothing will be made in all sizes, not only the tiny models' sizes. Demna Gvasalia of Balenciaga has said that he does not believe in fashion seasons or fashion week anymore.

I hope that the pandemic will catapult fashion into designing more and varied casual clothes, beautiful and easy to wear. As attached as I once was to my fancier clothes, I know that my lifestyle has changed irrevocably. I look in the museum of my closet in my unused city apartment—my own personal costume exhibit—and I see a symbol of a bygone era.

Though informal wear has been trending for a while, it had not become as dominant in the high fashion world as I expected. Throughout the pandemic, I was continually surprised by ads for gowns and fancy dresses with high heels. I wondered, "Who is wearing these clothes? Where? Why?"

For me the pandemic unleashed my ultimate preference for casual, comfortable clothes that are still beautiful and groomed-

looking. Clothes that fit our new informal, DIY, on-the-go
lifestyle. I am determined to adapt. Recently, I invested in a
variety of cute Bombas ankle socks in bright colors and patterns
and others in black with stickies on the bottom. The socks are
comfortable and fun for the long stretches of time I spend pad-
ding around my house. These socks are part of the cocoon experience. Their soft, downy, and cushioned construction feels like
wrapping a blanket around my whole self, ultimately triggering, yes, you guessed it . . . a protected, womb-like feeling.
My wardrobe now consists of different styles and colors of my
favorite jeans, appealing tops, silk blouses, and luscious chunky
sweaters, not to mention the socks! As cozy as I like my socks,
jeans have a sense of being comfortably bound and structured
that makes me feel alert, held together, and set up for presenting myself to the world in my higher-level thinking, in a way
that the ubiquitous stretch pants, with their merciful give to the
flesh, do not grant. Or I'll wear an informal but pretty dress
while I'm at the computer writing or meeting with a patient and
then transition out to lunch or dinner (in warm weather only,
of course) with friends. A dress that would do me proud if I ran
into someone I hadn't seen in a while and for whom I wanted
to look attractive. Fashion is about fantasy and transformation,
how we want to look, to feel, and to project ourselves in the
world. How can we create ourselves anew each day from our
raw, just-out-of-bed appearance into who we want to be and
how we want to feel? I want a cozy, attractive rag that makes
me feel good, especially now, in a moment of reduced access to
our usual supports. Fashion is like a little upper that provides
comfort and fresh vitality, as it helps me to adapt to our new
world.

The pandemic has subverted the old structures, the old norms, and thrown open the gates to changes that were already underway, in fashion, as in therapy and so many other fields. While there is no precedent or theory for how to proceed, we therapists need to adapt our current structure if we are to help our patients.

Seven months into the pandemic, Betsy informs me by text thirty minutes before the start of our session that she will not make it because she mistakenly scheduled her own clients during that time. Betsy has held this same time slot for several years now. She's a smart woman who is on top of her obligations. She goes on to explain via text that she thinks that beneath her mishap is her sense of shame about her body and a deeply held longing to hide away. I feel like the threads of our connection may be fraying. At the same time, I sense some trepidation from Betsy about her foray into the deeper, murkier, and scarier regions of her fears. In pre-pandemic times, I would not have carried on a discussion of such sensitive topics via text. I would suggest that we discuss the topics in person when we next see each other. Instead, I respond with a substantive text. Betsy needs such human engagement, recognition, and responsiveness (and in this moment she needs it via text). Her tenuous attempt to bridge the pandemic-size gap in our connection, because we never see each other in person anymore, shows new courage. When she engages with my response, I decide to call her. Betsy often doesn't pick up her phone. This time she does. I hear her relief as she receives the reassuring warmth and presence of my voice. She reiterates her theory about why she's avoiding our session. I tell her I understand and I normalize her anxiety, which increases the longer she is deprived of human contact with me and others. Betsy assures me that she will make our next session.

Normalizing my patients' anxieties was crucial during the pandemic. To not acknowledge the very real, anxiety-provoking circumstances of our everyday lives would have been akin to gaslighting my patients—an expression used to describe an act of psychological manipulation to undermine a person's experience of reality. The expression originates from a play and film titled *Gaslight*, about a deceitful husband who tries to convince his wife she is insane. When I normalized my patients' experiences, I validated their perceptions of the crisis. In addition to normalizing, generalizing, philosophizing, and even commiserating, too, became important tools in the therapeutic process, in a way I did not use them before. The heightened stress and shared crisis demanded that I come up to the surface of day-to-day reality and acknowledge its extraordinary, intense impact.

Pre-pandemic, I rarely signaled the kind of tacit encouragement to communicate significant emotional issues between sessions the way I did with Betsy. Now I feel that certain patients need this kind of support when their in-person contact with me is so attenuated. I needed to adapt so I could bridge the gaps caused by the ways we live our lives online. The surge in remote working and global travel (once it's fully safe) will continue to require such on-demand communication into the future.

The norms and structures of how I work have become more pliable, adaptable, and elastic. In psychotherapy, we call these norms and structures *the frame*. These are the parameters and guidelines each of us establishes around the borders of our work, within which we practice therapy. The pandemic changed the frame forever.

The Elastic Frame

The frame includes logistical and procedural matters, such as: How, where, and when do we meet—the office, phone, or Zoom? At 3:00 p.m.? How long are sessions? What is the fee and how and when is it paid? What is the cancellation and vacation policy? What is the therapist's role and the patient's role? For instance, for all the years of my practice prior to the pandemic, I told patients that once they came into my office and sat or lay down (more on that later), except for hello, I will wait until they start talking and I will say something only when I have something to say.

On the surface, the frame, as I've described it so far, appears to be a logistical and administrative device, and it literally is. Yet it stands for so much more. The frame is the metaphorical structure that contains the therapy and holds the therapeutic process together, the consistent and unvarying parameters. In a world where everything has been turned upside down, in therapy and elsewhere, the frame exists to provide a constant. In my personal (non-traditional) definition of the frame, the patient's unconscious life is part of the frame. Working with the unconscious (one of the most fundamental therapeutic techniques) is a constant. I think of my patients' internal landscape as a parallel to the physical spaces we have lost in the pandemic. And their internal landscape has shifted as a result of the pandemic and all else that is aswirl in the world in this time of profound change. I am part of the frame, too. This was always the case, but in an environment of exclusively remote work, this is truer than ever before. As patients and I meet in a remote landscape, each in our different (and often changing) geographical locations, untethered from our mutual physical presences in the office, I am a constant for the patient (as, of course, she is for me).

With this expansive view of the frame in mind, I'd like to embark on a deeper exploration of the ways in which the logistical and therapeutic elements of the frame changed and are changing—the patients' conscious and unconscious needs and the ways in which I am working with them.

While the evolving modifications were triggered by the pandemic, we have been moving toward these changes for a while now. In our increasingly complicated, global world of constant mobility and a proliferation of ways to meet and communicate, therapists had begun already to realize that there wasn't just one way to practice therapy. Though virtual therapy was the only option for many months, even as things open, the choice of whether to meet in the office, on the phone, or on video will be permanently on offer. The pandemic sealed the internet dominance that was already insinuating itself into our work and social life. Even in therapy now, one of the bastions of human-to-human personal contact, the need to, or expectation that we will, meet in person has been eroded.

The frame has become elastic. When asked whether it is better to be strict or lenient in disciplining one's children, the famous pediatrician Dr. Spock said either is fine as long as there are some limits within a lenient family and there is some flexibility within a strict family; so too, the frame. What matters is not how traditional or open the frame is, or how strict or loose it is. What matters is that there is a frame and that it is lenient enough to adapt to the pandemic and how the world will be next. And that it is strict enough to keep patient and therapist safe and the work of the therapy effective. Has the frame expanded or narrowed? Maybe. What we know for sure is that the frame has changed. What matters most is that there is a frame that establishes the conditions, norms, and expectations of our work with patients. The elasticity of the frame is its ability to be responsive to the patient and our environmental conditions. The frame of old was rigid (though like all aspects of analytic therapy, it has been softening over the years), responsive only to theory and conditions that may no longer be relevant. The frame must be stretched. As with any elasticity, our challenge is to stay alert to the possible breaking point. Because, ultimately, the frame's purpose is to create safe conditions for the most effective therapy.

Let's look at some of the specifics of the frame.

Billing and Email

Billing is an example of a basic issue that has changed in my practice as a result of the pandemic. I used to give all my patients paper bills that I wrote out by hand and gave to them in person, in their session. They then gave me a check. I managed this bit of the frame in this way to make the money and billing a therapeutic subject. My billing was more personal because I solicited payment in a personal manner. Now I bill by email, and I am paid through Zelle.

Prior to the pandemic, I never used email with patients, unless they absolutely had to send me a document. I worked that way because I did not want to miss or feel overwhelmed by an email from a patient that arrives on a day when I have one too many to handle. Email brings the risk of an open spigot, an exchange of messages that becomes a session between sessions.

Email all too easily encourages an ever flowing stream of communication, without beginning or end, which subverts one of the prime purposes of a therapy session—to capture important nuances of information related to the patient. The framework of my email policy was a way of organizing the overabundant flow of information in our lives today. In my experience, email can be akin to on-demand breastfeeding. Cutting it off can be delicate. My policy ensured that I kept my communications with patients personal, as *I to thou*, and not *I to computer*. I revised and am revising my policy on the fly, as circumstances demand.

My new patient Carol is too anguished to tell me some important background to her feelings of shame and insecurity. Her feelings inhibit her ability to talk in our sessions. Carol hands me a letter after one of her first few sessions. In it is a moving story, with some history behind her feelings. I respond by email because I want to respond quickly before seeing her again, thus establishing that now email correspondence is acceptable in my practice. I keep my response brief, validating, and contained. A day later, I feel so moved by this new patient's trust in me, someone who is still a relative stranger, that I call her. In this way, I make contact and signal that I understand the delicate and important nature of what she has communicated. I judge that she will respond best if I keep my call understated. She responds with warmth, consideration, and relief. My revised outreach policy yields fruit.

Session Length, Predictability, and Endings

Session length is another frame basic. In this, I have mostly kept with my usual session length of forty-five minutes for individual sessions and sixty or seventy-five minutes for couples and families, though I am more flexible than before.

Session predictability is another important element. One of the major purposes and provisions of the frame is that it offers a reliable and dedicated structure for the patient. During a session, they know that they can count on the therapist's undivided, undistracted attention and interest in the patient.

Frank tells me how grounding he finds the timed regularity of our sessions. He says he orients himself in part around the predictability of our time together, especially at a time when there is very little else to mark off days, hours, and places.

Carol, who can be quite ambivalent about the whole therapy process, tells me that she so values this time when she has my undivided attention, to think and speak about herself and whatever she wants. She calls it a privilege.

My patients' responses to the sanctity of their sessions shines a light on the importance of a reliable frame. The work would lose a crucial portion of its sense of safety and trustworthiness if the therapist, or patient, for that matter, is frequently canceling or rescheduling. And this need for predictability certainly extends to other aspects of the frame.

In this way, the therapeutic endeavor shares aspects of parenting. Without in any way suggesting that my patients are children or childish, it is also true that just as children need a reliable parent who will basically be there wherever and whenever, so too patients require this solidity from their therapist. With patients for whom that element of parenting was missing from their childhood, it is especially important to find it in the person of the therapist, in order to feel safe enough to divulge one's vulnerabilities. And by the way, the same holds true for a parent's emotional stability. If the parent's moods are unpredictable and labile, the child will experience the same sense of danger and absence, as if the parent is frequently physically unavailable. Part of my work is to be available on a reliable schedule.

While length and predictability of sessions has not changed, what has changed is the endings. *End. Ending. Ended.* The words alone strike anxiety in my heart. Oh, how I hate them, especially an ending with someone I love. My husband says I have difficulty with transitions. It's not transitions that are hard for me. I am highly adaptive to new situations. I hate endings!

I love my patients. The very fact that they come to me, put their trust in me, bare their souls to me, and tell me things they do not entrust to anyone else makes me bond deeply to them. I feel a loving responsibility toward them. I feel honored to hold their secrets and to be privy to their true, inner selves.

Yes, they can anger, hurt, and frustrate me at times, some more than others. But that comes with loving them. It means they matter enough to touch me. It's worth it to me to stick with them despite their occasional difficult behavior. It is my job to understand the vulnerable underbelly that causes them to be difficult. This is another aspect of my work that has elements like parenting. Your kids can make you angry, but you don't drop them because of it. As therapists, we try to understand what is going on with our patients, to find a way to discuss what they are experiencing, to find the right way to respond in a way that will ultimately benefit them, so that the patient learns and grows from the experience.

All to say, ending sessions has always been hard for me. I am not a therapist who cuts people off midsentence when their time is up, as a few of my own therapists have done. Nor do I find it easy to do so when a patient is in an emotional moment or developing an idea at the end of the session. I try my best to let them finish their thought. Then I end the session as tactfully as possible. I am highly invested in the success and well-being of my patients. When there is pathos and intensity in the session, it signals the patient's engagement in the work in a way that feels like we have created something positive together. In psychoanalysis, we call this co-construction. It can feel like striking gold. I want to see where it leads. At the very least, I want to dignify the moment. So I am loath to cut that off.

Endings were even harder during the pandemic and even now. My best guess is that the feeling is connected to the tenuousness of the electronic connection, combined with the open-ended nature of the pandemic and recovery period. We don't know when this disruption will fully end. As of this writing, I still hadn't seen any of my patients in person except for one, one time. There is an uncertainty, longing, and wistfulness that hovers beneath the surface of even the most successful of our interactions.

While I am awed by how well remote therapy is working, that the hard and emotional work of therapy is getting done and change is happening, there is a subplot that emerges in certain elements, like my difficulty in ending sessions. Most of us are living with a pandemic-driven conscious—or, at least, subconscious—sense of uncertainty about the state of the world. We don't know what our world will look like next year. Even as the pandemic eases, we wonder whether we or our loved ones will get sick or possibly even die from one of the new, more virulent strains of COVID. From the profound to the mundane, radical changes were happening in the blink of an eye. We wondered what would happen to jobs, businesses, and work life. I wondered when I could get my computer guy to fix my electronic problems, and I still need to decide what to do about the two idle offices on which I pay rent. Will school go back to how it was before? My eldest son recently got married—a pandemic wedding for fifteen people. As happy as I was for him, I felt sadness, too. He and his wife say they will have a larger celebration later. Will they? When? My middle son is engaged and waiting until spring 2022, on the hope that we will be in a postpandemic world by then.

All this uncertainty fostered a heightened sense of fragility. I wanted to hold on when a patient's session was coming to an end. And the uncertainty drags on.

There's No Office Anymore

Then there's one of the hottest frame topics—what does not coming to my *office* look like? To begin with, I have patients call me, or in the case of Zoom, they have to proactively link into the meeting. They initiate the contact, just as it was them who made the effort to come to my office. Following each other on the phone, FaceTime, Zoom, or however else we are meeting, while we sit, lie down, walk, move inside or outside, is now part of the structure of the work. From session to session, we may follow each other from office to home or from one geographic locale to another. While I do not bring up my patients' choices of venue or position directly, in some instances, I will try to raise frame issues. I might, for example, ask a patient how their new setting feels or what it means to them. I don't want to raise the topic in a way that disrupts our process. I am still figuring out how and when it might be clinically useful.

What about that infamous piece of psychoanalytic furniture, the couch? The couch is about more than just not having the therapist in the patient's sightline. The couch is about the experience of free-associating while in a prone position. The sense of privacy and relaxation that the couch may induce can facilitate the therapy process. Where does it fit in the elastic frame? In my brick-and-mortar practice, I always gave my patients the choice. I never required someone to sit or lie down. Recognizing that the decision to lie down is a big one, I would first discuss the patient's feelings and the pros and cons. Before the pandemic, most of my patients *sat* in my office. A few lay on the couch and fewer still made different choices on different days, a mode of behavior we discussed ahead of time. As therapist, it is my job to make the decision itself an issue, to explore why any given patient makes the choice they do. The issue speaks differently now, to be sure. Some of my colleagues have taken for granted that their patients will or should continue to lie or sit as they did in the office prior to the pandemic. I see telephone meetings as couch-like, though not exactly, of course. One colleague has said that she has established a virtual couch protocol. The patients she was seeing on the couch in her office are continuing their sessions on a couch.

For most though, the pressures that patients are under to adapt and find a private space that accommodates phone and screen work takes precedence over insisting on the use of the couch. Like me, many of my colleagues have not insisted, either. We have yet to figure out how that might disrupt the analytic process. We are all making it up as we go along.

Without my office, patients are sometimes stressed looking for their therapy space. In addition, some of the aspects of phone work, as I mentioned, mimic the couch. We do not see each other. There is a physical turning away from one another. It is interesting to me that so many of the people who meet me on-screen do so from their bed or from a reclining position on a couch. What does it feel like to interact with your therapist from bed? Does that create a kind of intimacy that did not exist in my office?

All these issues of location, space, and body position are concepts Freud was aware of when he first proposed the use of the couch for patients. He did it both because it was too hard for him to be looked at all day and scrutinized for his response, but also because lying on a couch induces a more relaxed and regressed state in a patient. This state helps the therapist and patient alike to reach deeper inside the mind. Patients who are tightly wound or feel easiest when they are in control, including those who have an obsessive bent, derive special benefit from the loosening effect of the couch. They may be benefiting from remote work for the same reason. Or the opposite. People are varied in their needs even within the same diagnosis. It is too early to say for sure.

One thing I haven't heard anybody address is the sensation of materiality and physicality that is integral to sitting in an office with actual furniture and objects and people with physical clothes and possessions like a purse or backpack, shoes, watches, or jewelry. This lack of human and object presence and physical sensation is one more way in which we are losing the materiality of the physical world. I cannot say that I know all the effects of this loss. There is a feeling of being grounded or rooted in the world that is ebbing away.

How location, movement, and the therapy space impact therapeutic technique has not been widely written about. Now, they are of enormous concern to therapists and, perhaps less overtly, to our patients. No doubt any answers I give here will evolve over time, as conditions change. The pandemic has catalyzed shifts that were already underway pre-pandemic, as well as the pandemic-specific changes. I, and most people I know, believe that work, possibly including therapeutic work, has changed forever now that people have discovered that they can work just as effectively remotely. I know several therapists who say they will never go into an office again, and plan to work exclusively remote.

One big, obvious change for patients and therapists alike is working in highly personal spaces, so much different than the classic, theoretically *neutral* offices therapists worked in pre-pandemic. Whether our offices were ever truly neutral is debatable. *Professional* is probably a better word. Like many of my peers, I am working from several locations, different rooms and outdoor spaces, and even different geographical locations. So far, I have worked from a Manhattan apartment, a Westchester house, and a Martha's Vineyard house. I have worked from a home office, a bedroom, a dining room, a sunroom, and from outside spaces, such as my back patio, a secluded outdoor space behind the pandemic-shuttered public library in Martha's Vineyard, and walking on deserted streets or in quiet, private parts of Central Park. How do my patients feel about this? Mostly, I do not know. I listen for references and allusions to my *space*. To proactively ask about their reactions could be interruptive of the therapeutic process. I'll say more later about this enormous issue of self-disclosure. I have received small expressions of curiosity about my surroundings. For example, when I walk outside and a loud car drives by, a patient may ask where I am. I have chosen to answer directly. I don't want to mimic an experience I never enjoyed as a patient. Some of my former analysts answered any direct questions with silence. Boy, did that silence used to shut me down. It did not feel like it helped the analytic process. My personal credo is to keep things open in a way that facilitates the patient's free associations.

Some of the places my patients are when we meet include their bedrooms (many are lying in bed), their home offices, their living rooms, an outdoor patio, even their cars (when it is the only place where they can find privacy from family members or office mates). Sometimes I don't immediately know where they are calling from, since, like me, they change locations.

Many of my colleagues have remarked that they are gaining information about their patients from seeing their home surroundings. I don't feel like I see enough on-screen. There is the occasional exception.

One day the computer screen opens on what seems to be a different home office from the one in which she usually meets with me. It has some similarities to her usual office, so I'm not sure at first. I notice a window wrapping around behind her that looks out on a solid gray panorama. As I register some confusion and surprise, Emma explains to me that she is in her vacation home. She seems to assume that I understand that I am seeing an enormous, unobstructed view of the ocean. I imagine, too, that her misapprehension comes from Emma's belief that I too do or could have a house so situated. I have just witnessed one of the perks of Emma's income status. Prior to now, my knowledge of her wealth was more abstract. I ask myself whether this witnessing provides me with more insight. My experience is akin to seeing a play mounted onstage versus an unstaged reading of the script. A quality of her life comes alive in a new way.

Moving to virtual therapy has been an enormous shift. So, I will devote these next pages to the topic.

Remote Therapy

Pre-pandemic, I certainly had the occasional session by phone or video, when a patient was traveling, sick, or otherwise indisposed. That frame was radically different from always working remotely, as I'm doing now. When the pandemic started, I gave all my patients the choice of whether they wanted to meet by phone (voice only), FaceTime, or Zoom.

While there are several factors that determine which venue I prefer, the main deciding factor for me is what works best for the patient. If a choice of device works well for them, the therapy will go better and that makes my job easier (and more enjoyable). I get enormous joy from knowing a patient is benefiting from their therapy and using me in a way that helps them. Yes, folks, this is using, but a good kind of using.

The factors that sway me toward video include: Have I met this person before? Is this a patient who has signaled the importance of seeing me? Is it someone who tends to be vigilant? Has the balance tipped too far toward phone? Do I have a comfortable place to do video work? Does this person speak fluently and easily? How have I been feeling recently? Factors that sway me toward phone include: Is this someone who experiences a lot of shame? Who privileges their privacy? Is this someone who prefers to not be seen? Do I need more physical freedom of movement? In spite of these considerations, some of my patients have surprised me, choosing the opposite mode from what I would have guessed for them.

At the very outset of the pandemic, each person (including couples and families) made immediate and sure-sounding choices between phone, FaceTime, and Zoom. This speed and clarity of choice was striking, especially for those patients who are often riddled with ambivalence and indecisiveness in other parts of their lives.

Together we have been discovering the benefits and drawbacks of ongoing virtual therapy. On the immediate plus side, I am thrilled, as are many of my patients, with the newfound freedom. We can work from home or really anywhere. Every day feels like a snow day. I have the luxury of sleeping a little later in the morning. I glide seamlessly between domestic duties, my writing, other work projects, and meeting with patients.

During the summer of 2020, I worked from Martha's Vineyard. Instead of spending three all-too-short weeks and a few weekends in one of my favorite places in the world, I had several glorious, indulgent months. Some days I worked from an upstairs office flooded with the bright beach light. Other days, I was ensconced on a screened-in porch, sheltered in the cool shade and breeze. The warm, thick air of summer was set against the backdrop of the grass, flowers, and pool. Occasionally our neighborhood family of deer appeared in the yard.

Most importantly, my patients discovered that they can get perfectly good therapy without leaving their house. Many are very comfortable online and on the phone. They transitioned from in-person to remote and were able to continue to reflect deeply on themselves. In some cases, our work has been more profound with the distance. I have new patients I've never met in person. Even they have felt comfortable enough to plunge right into the kind of personal content, which dances around the unconscious, almost from the moment we met each other's virtual images. I am astounded by how well virtual therapy works. Yet I continue to feel that something precious is lost.

Navigating the new dimensions is an evolving challenge. The different devices present their unique positives and negatives.

Therapy by Phone

When I gave them the choice, most of my patients chose the phone, at least at first.

From passing statements they have made, I've discerned that many of my patients who chose the phone liked the freedoms it gave them to move around, to be in odd locations, to find privacy (either from me or from the people they live with—some go out to their cars for sessions, as I've mentioned). The phone can be intimate. There is no delay in the transmission of sound. Our voices are in each other's ears, close and snug, even as we walk and move around while we talk to each other. For me the ability to move, even go for a walk, while listening feels wonderful and liberating.

Some chose the phone because they did not want to be seen, or they wanted the freedom to be schlumpy, to wear what they wanted, or they were self-conscious about their appearance. When they are not seen, some patients can more easily share shameful or guilt-ridden emotions and thoughts.

In my office, pre pandemic, Linda was often struck with bouts of self-consciousness. Now, she speaks more fluently than before. Her confidence has grown from within. She tells me that our meetings (as well as her phone dates with a new man) have loosened her inhibitions. She tells me that in person she feels uncomfortable with the occasional silence and becomes self-conscious that she is being looked at. On the phone, she feels the freedom that comes with not being looked at.

Yet there are downsides to not seeing each other. What not seeing one another means for each patient differs. This is a question that analytic therapists should constantly ask themselves and their patients. As a profession, we don't take any information about our patients for granted. Every response to any change in the frame is grist for the mill.

Pre-pandemic, Betsy would lie on the couch in my office, facing me, rather than away from me, as is the psychoanalytic standard. Seeing me allows her to satisfy her vigilance, to make sure I am there, to track me, monitor my attention, and be sure that I am not running out on her. When Betsy was elementary school age, she lived with her father. Her father got fed up with getting her up and out of the house in time to catch the school bus. He took to leaving the house on school mornings while she was still asleep. She would wake up to an empty house, the school bus long gone and no way to get to school. This situation was just one of the ways her father abandoned his young daughter, causing panic, shame, loneliness, and a deep distrust of caregivers and authorities. Her feelings are particularly poignant to me because Betsy's father was a therapist, who often used his knowledge of psychology as a weapon to criticize his daughter.

Betsy's memory of missed school buses is what we call a *screen memory* in psychoanalysis. This is a memory that consolidates multiple similar experiences into one symbolic memory. One of my favorite cartoons in *The Agony in the Kindergarten*, by William Steig, depicts a young child sitting at the dinner table in front of a mountain of mashed potatoes she is supposed to finish. The task is making her feel sick and overwhelmed. What Steig's drawing captures is a typical screen memory that any adult might experience (probably even Steig). We call this a screen memory because the plate of mashed potatoes may have happened or it may not have. The memory may be a blend of several different, yet similar, events. What the memory captures is a theme from childhood. In the mashed potato memory, the theme is having things pushed on you that you didn't want or that were too much. Screen memories capture experiences that make a deep impression and have a lot of meaning. They can reflect or indicate scars and unfulfilled needs. In Betsy's case, she has an abiding, unfulfilled need to trust that important people in her life will not leave her high and dry. Not seeing me, either in person or over video, taps into Betsy's school bus screen memory. Yet her desire to hide her pandemic appearance (less perfectly turned out than her usual) is stronger than her need to see me. So we continue by phone.

During one phone session, Susan says, "I need to block out distractions now in order to think deeply about myself. In your office, no one is there interrupting us or making demands or noises. I can see your facial expressions. That makes you more real. Depending on how I'm feeling about the topic or on that particular day, your realness can help me confide more or it can add to my resistance. You feel more anonymous to me on the phone. That can inhibit me at first, but once I relax into it, the anonymity actually helps me block out distractions and allows me to reveal my inner thoughts." Susan then spoke with a new and rare frankness about her husband and her marriage.

The phone allows Susan a reassuring sense of autonomy and freedom. She doesn't feel like she has to show up for me, as she has to show up for her mother, regardless of Susan's own needs. The phone allows Susan to make our therapy sessions her own, instead of something she has to do for me.

Hannah is pregnant for the first time. She conceived two weeks before the first cases of COVID-19 appeared in New York. Her early pregnancy took place when there was little known about the virus and how it was transmitted. It seemed as if every move could threaten her and her unborn baby. Terrified and confused, she didn't even know how or whether she could get to the doctor's office safely. Worse still, her partner had to quarantine away from her because of his hospital job.

Over the years, prior to the pregnancy, she had lost an excessive amount of weight. On video, her face appears gaunt. Is her weight healthy enough for the pregnancy? The fact that she has not said anything about her weight (as she has numerous times over past years), and the fact that she is hiding her body suggests to me that she is not happy with her physical state. I know this is an issue for her. While she still identifies as a beautiful woman, she is often rumpled and ashamed of her appearance. She expresses envy of the beautiful women she sees on the streets in New York City, and what she imagines is their disciplined, *get it done* approach to their fitness and beauty routines.

Even before the pandemic, she had trouble getting out of bed and out of the house to make it to a session. She was already coming to my office in person infrequently.

She works as a film editor, so she has worked from home for quite some time. Yet I know, too, that she had extreme difficulty not ever seeing me in person. She could not express her difficulty because she perceived her need as shameful. This was easier for her to express pre-pandemic, when she was the one who made the frequent decision not to come in to my office. When seeing me in person was not even an option, it was harder for her to get a handle on her desire to see me, much less express it.

Hannah was not my only patient having difficulty with our physical absence from each other. Like Hannah, few expressed their feelings to me in words. Their actions told me they miss me. As with Hannah, I was initially surprised when I detected that Betsy missed our in-person contact. Like Hannah, Betsy becomes easily exhausted by the exigencies of everyday life, tasks, obligations, jobs, commutes, and demands, which have always blighted her everyday life. Both women are exquisitely sensitive to the winds of events both external and internal. They are frequently laid flat by bodily aches and pains and emotional storms, as well as despondency and pessimism. Pre-pandemic, Betsy would often opt for the phone as a way to relieve the pressure of commuting to see me. The exigencies of the pandemic feel even more pronounced for them.

By two months after shelter-in-place started and we were restricted to working exclusively on the phone, both of Hannah and Betsy's speech had become more halting and fainter than their usual fluent expressions. They were starting to cancel

sessions last minute, even when they knew they would have to
pay for the session (an element of the frame that did not change).
They had intended to show up but *couldn't* do it at the last minute. I know that the more they don't show up to sessions, the
more they don't see me, the more abandoned and hopeless they
will feel. This is what they do in the rest of their lives with boy-
friends, with jobs. Then they will feel that they were rejected
once again. Betsy dealt with painful dissatisfactions in her
romantic relationship with a suitable man. Hannah had the
courage to face painful truths about her ambivalence toward her
pregnancy. Most women feel at least a hint of ambivalence at
some point, even toward pregnancies they are strongly attached to. But they inhibit their awareness and certainly their
expressions of such feelings. Right before I delivered Zach, my
oldest, I full on panicked that I'd made a mistake. That as
passionately as I wanted him, I wasn't ready.

To interrupt this cycle is delicate. Neither of them wanted
to be seen much during our session. Yet not being seen interfered with their processes. I wanted to let them know, in the
most supportive way possible, what they were doing to themselves when they avoided contact. When Hannah brings up
frustration with our meetings or veiled anger with me, then I
can bring up the idea that not seeing me might be difficult, tying
that back to past experiences of felt and real abandonment.

Months later Hannah gave birth to a healthy baby girl to
whom she devoted herself with great joy and tenderness. The
baby is thriving. For Hannah, the process of naming her fears
and facing her doubts helped her to accept her imperfections as
a mother. She engaged with feelings that had previously felt

inadmissible to her. Understanding that her feelings were normal, was a bitter yet liberating process, which allowed her to tolerate the rigorous demands of mothering with considerably less conflict and anxiety.

When Betsy talks about uneasy feelings during the pandemic, frustrations with not seeing people, feeling cut off and forgotten, and the sameness of being home all the time (all while disavowing her need to socialize and see people and her real sense of relief at having few social obligations), then I can bring up her ambivalence about closeness and explain that I think doing at least occasional FaceTime sessions might relieve some of her sense of being untethered from the warm bonds of closeness to others.

Another patient who missed me, but could not express it, was Ellie, a patient who had always made it crystal clear that meeting virtually was not an option for her, that she needed to see me in person. Ellie, too, skipped more sessions than usual, shortened sessions and alternated between giving herself over to a new depth of work and needing more than her usual encouragement to talk during sessions. Ellie needs to see how I react to her. She wants to know whether I am interested, agree, disagree, think she's stupid, smart, or anything else. There's a bigger factor driving her need that's more nebulous and all-encompassing. She's trying to find her image in my eyes as a way to consolidate her own sense of self. She could never complete this consolidation in her childhood, because she could not find the understanding, acceptance, and validation that she needed from her caregivers. Finding oneself in a caregiver's eyes is a necessary aspect of forming a confident sense of self in the world and feeling comfortable in one's own skin.

Here let me take another brief detour to set some therapeutic context. Talk therapy can stir up all kinds of feelings in the patient, both positive and negative, many of which are directed toward the therapist. Feelings, like those Ellie has for me, are indeed real and sometimes passionately felt. But all good therapists know that these sincere feelings most often have their roots in a patient's childhood feelings, wishes, and fears toward their family members and other significant figures in their life, the very people who shaped their perspectives on relationships and life. As the figure of the therapist gains importance for a patient, many of these old feelings get redirected onto the therapist. It is important that this transference of feelings get recognized and explored together by therapist and patient at a time and in a way that is helpful and mutative.

I am moved by my patients' inability or unwillingness to tell me how hard it is to not see me. I can see how each one strains to hold up their end of the bargain, so to speak, in this new way of working. It is almost as if each of them feels that to confide their sense of loss would disrupt or end the treatment. I also have to consider the shame that might be involved for them in exposing their missing me, without knowing how I feel about not seeing them. Their fantasies about how I feel about the loss of their physical presences, their desire (non-sexual) for my presence, their shame, frustration, helplessness, and anger may all feel too sensitive to reveal. There's a risk of triggering past traumatic experiences with caregivers who were absent or unavailable at tender ages. This is one of the trickier moments in treatment, when creative, healing work can be done in the transference. We are called to deal with the risk therapeutically. If we do not handle the moment well (and sometimes the patient will never tolerate the situation no matter what the therapist says or does), then the transference may feel intolerable or too real, causing the patient to have a setback or to leave.

I normally hold back early in a session, because I want to see what the patient brings in that day, unhampered by my agenda. But right out of the box, I hear Ellie's hesitance and I want to catch the moment. After many years of our working together, I sense that if we were in the same room together, my physical presence would provide the reassurance she needs to sit in silence and collect her thoughts. Sitting in silence can be terrifying for many. I struggle with it at times. Ellie can tolerate silence well in person, but I sense that the phone is challenging her comfort level. I tell Ellie right at the beginning of our session that I think she is having a hard time with the phone. She answers with an enthusiastic yes. She seems relieved that I notice and she does not have to put it into words. Like many patients, she wants to know what we can do about it. She is despondent that there seems to be nothing we can do at the moment. Like any good analytic therapist, I tell her we can discuss practical solutions, but that first could we explore what is so hard about not seeing me in person. At this point in her therapy process, Ellie knows that this kind of exploration can yield insights, so she goes along with it. I follow the twists and turns of her thinking process until I see that we have reached a point at which it finally feels right to tell her what had been striking me for years. By now she has practically told me so herself. All I have to do is package the insight in an interpretation that she can swallow, digest, and use to organize and shed light on the morass of inchoate feelings swarming in her head.

I say, "You want to find yourself in my mind. You want to know how I view you and react to you—in essence what and how I think of you as a person." Again, I get an enthusiastic yes. Ellie had been distrustful of the therapeutic process and therefore me as a therapist throughout the first couple of years of her therapy. Now, at last, we are able to relate her experience of missing me and my reactions to her to her mistrust of her mother and the way she wanted to save the have-nots in the world, even as she could not relate to her own daughter. She speaks about how alone and frustrating that felt to her. Having used this little crisis point as an opportunity for deeper understanding, I bring up the practical suggestion of trying out FaceTime. Hesitantly at first and then with more conviction, she agrees to try it. Though it is awkward for her on our first attempt, she is reassured by seeing me. Over time she relaxes into it.

Even in these evolving times, as therapist, it's better that I not tell my patients that I miss seeing them in person. There's a good reason for this. To say, "I miss you," is an evocative emotion to express to a person and can produce a range of reactions in the patient, from feeling special to feeling obligated. The expression can be a burden that requires reciprocity from them, which risks being more about the therapist's needs than the patient's needs. There are certainly exceptions, when it is helpful to the goal of the therapy.

I recognize, too, how hard it is for patients to deal with the asymmetry of being dependent on their therapist, whereas, in their view, their therapist is not dependent on them. What I do more of these days is let my patients know through my affect that I wish I could see them in person. I am extra present.

Dedicated. Through this presence and dedication, I communicate my engagement, my warmth and love. I communicate that each patient matters. I had one patient who went through a big surgery lately and another whose spouse had surgery. In both cases, I asked for news of the outcome of the surgeries.

These days I may send a follow-up note to a patient in between sessions, if I have something brief but important to tack onto our last session. I am stretching myself to compensate for the ways in which the pandemic has diminished our contact. At the same time, in this new frame, I need to stay vigilant to not let my own needs interfere with good practice. I don't want to reenact ways in which their caregivers would not let them separate, for example. My patients' therapy cannot be about me and my needs, because I would be unwittingly reenacting a conflict of theirs, a conflict that would be important for them to express out loud so we could work toward their understanding in our sessions. This is how patients come to have free will over their own behavior and choices.

With a few patients, the distance created by the phone moves me to cut to the chase sooner than I might otherwise. Ideally, as therapist you want a patient to come to an insight or revelation on their own. It means more to them that way. The therapist's skill is to ask the right questions to open the door to a patient's own awareness. Patients may provide us with all the information. We therapists connect the dots or propose an interpretation for how to understand or make sense of their output.

Sixty-five-year-old Kathy continues to talk to me about her loneliness and feelings of being devalued at work as she ages and faces the possibility of falling ill. She also talks about her ongoing struggles with fears from earlier in her life, those of financial inadequacy, of being alone and in need. Kathy is an effective employee and well liked by friends, students, and coworkers. She expresses her sense of aloneness even as she also describes her popularity coupled with her dread of social events. She sounds increasingly despairing. Beneath her words, I can hear that she knows she has to do something. I cut to the chase and tell her that she may need to force herself to act, even if she doesn't feel like it. She needs to put herself in social interactions and take up her many invitations way more than she naturally wants to. All the while, she and I can explore and make sense of her resistance and anxieties. But first, "Act!" I fear that my little push will be unwanted and resisted. Instead, she responds with a palpable sense of relief. Kathy heartily agrees it is time for action. My phone-induced boldness is effective.

What about my experience? What's the phone like for a therapist? I loved it. At first. Technically, phone communication was smooth, with none of the glitches of Zoom and FaceTime. In comparison to screen meetings, the phone feels non-mechanical. There is the intimacy I've mentioned of having someone's voice snuggled in your ear. And, as I've also mentioned, I love the ability to work and move around at the same time and to look and dress however I feel. But about two months into shelter-in-place, I began to miss the physical presence of my patients. I didn't miss any one thing in particular, not their facial expressions or body language specifically, though those aspects of human behavior are certainly part of it. I missed something more amorphous, which I think of as the heat of a human presence.

Some years ago, for example, I began to notice that during sessions with male patients, my body temperature goes up slightly, even with a man I am not attracted to. This is called a galvanic skin response, a measure of electrodermal activity—in other words, how the sweat glands respond to a stimulus. Two months into the pandemic, I began to experience a sense of restlessness and deprivation. The response is less pronounced with patients who speak easily and fluidly, who are introspective and engaged with their own internal life, or at least trying. But with patients who have difficulty disengaging from extended factual narratives of the events of their life, without linking them to their deeper personal and psychic meanings, phone work can be extra challenging and lead to moments of sluggishness and frustration for me.

What does my patients' initial overwhelming choice of the phone over video say about our culture's assumption that video is best? Technology development assumes that we would always choose to see each other. My patients disproved this assumption in their initial choices. As time has worn on, Ellie revised her phone choice and switched to video. Two other patients, whose work with me predated the pandemic, chose to have one video session to fulfill a visual fix.

Therapy by Video

As the pandemic settled in for the longer haul, video became a more popular choice for my patients. I now do about half and half between video and phone. Some of my existing patients and all my new patients see me on FaceTime or Zoom. With my new patients, the phone option has barely come up. Having never met in person, we want to be able to see each other.

In our fifth session, the new patient Carol, who has only ever met with me on Zoom, mentions that we do not know the opportunity costs of never having met each other in person. This is undeniably true. We try to figure out if we could have one of our sessions while taking a walk. She has recently gotten a dog and suggests she might bring the dog with her. The issue of our doing a walking session surfaces as she is painting a picture of some of her social anxieties. Her comments strike me as a poignant wish for more human connection. How might she have been different, perhaps more relaxed and forthcoming, if we had met in person? The impact of remote therapy is so complicated to understand. We start to discuss the how, where, and when of a walking session, but she ends our conversation before we resolve any of the logistics. I bring the idea up another day, in an unobtrusive way, just to let her know that I have not forgotten and am not avoiding the topic. She does not pursue my opening.

Another day, after meeting exclusively on Zoom, Carol calls in for a phone session. We have an extensive discussion about the relative pros and cons of video versus phone versus in person in my hypothetical office. We talk about how unbound it is to meet in cyberspace. Carol says it would be easier for her to meet in my office. Her reason touches on one of my main observations and conundrums about practicing virtual therapy. She tells me that meeting in cyberspace feels to her like it makes us equal, symmetric. The symmetry of our roles makes it more difficult for her to conform to my practice policies and habits. She believes that if we were to meet in my concrete office, it would be easier to conform to the asymmetry of our roles, to abide by my authority and therefore the frame.

All of Carol's comments pull me further into her inner world. My desire to know this young woman grows, as does my curiosity about what makes her tick and what brings her to see me.

Then, in March 2021, Carol reaches out to me and says she wants to meet outside for a session. So, we do. It is a warm winter day at about fifty degrees. We sit in sweaters, our coats lying by our side just in case we need them. We wear masks and sit side by side on two separate benches, by a pond covered in melting ice, ringed by snowy trees and grass. She has brought her dog, too. And the pup sleeps quietly under Carol's bench. We can barely hear the nearby road. We talk for an hour. I have done this type of session several times now with different patients. The calm surroundings promote introspection, a live version of the large framed photo in my office, of placid, blue lake water with a small boat in the middle. The photo image evokes for me the forays I make with my patients, beneath the surface of their consciousness, into the deep waters of their mental life. If at all practical, I recommend this as a way to do therapy, even post-pandemic.

I was reminded of the pleasure of the performance aspect of upping my dressing and grooming game a bit, in the way that one presents oneself for in-person, work-related get-togethers, in the world beyond my house.

Among my patients who started out choosing FaceTime or Zoom, I sense one of the reasons is that they want to be seen. For some of the women, this manifests in an attention to their appearance and allure.

When the Zoom screen opens up, I am taken aback. My first view of my new patient is of a slender, beautiful woman, lying on a divan outside, in a bikini. She is surrounded by large, plush, and colorful pillows, ensconced in the exotic decor of what looks like a Moroccan riad, by the side of a swimming pool. I wonder what's going on. Why is she dressed and posed so seductively for her first meeting with me? I do not ask her, knowing that if we agree to work together going forward, I will be alert to information that answers this question.

Bella is not my only patient to appear scantily dressed during our sessions. Franny used to show up in person in provocative outfits and brag about her power over men. She has extended her flirtatious manner of dressing to the virtual platform. I wonder whether Franny is simply reflecting the cultural norms of the European country she comes from, or whether this manner of dress is purely personal. I am also alerted to the awkward eventuality that the camera angle on FaceTime can catch my own bustline when I sit in certain positions. I remind myself to guard against that and reflect on what a strange new factor that is to contend with in the virtual world of therapy.

One of the things therapists agonize over is how to bring up a topic that announces itself in the room (even the virtual room), but which might be shaming if we bring it up. On some occasions, I might bring it up from another angle, looking for narcissism or grandiosity in other aspects of the patient's personality. With Franny, she hardly responds when I comment on her manner. I understand that her cleavage and bragging about men come from her unconscious. How and when to bring up the unconscious is a highly delicate craft and I always want to avoid doing it too abruptly. For this same reason, I did not ask Bella about her attire, either, choosing instead to wait for the answer to emerge in our sessions.

I notice that my own affect is different in the untethered virtual spaces. There are times in virtual sessions, when I find that I'm upping my expressiveness with a patient, chatting more, nodding, saying yes, or amplifying the coloratura of my responses in other ways. I realize that I am compensating for the cooling effect of a computer screen. There is a reason television is called the Cool Medium. We are communicating with each other as TV show to TV show. The flattening, neutralizing effect of remote work necessitates a heightened affective presence from the therapist. I watch myself slip into this mode, even occasionally explicitly voicing encouragement and approval to a patient, a practice that is a no-no in traditional psychoanalytic talk therapy, often for good clinical reasons. The mere physical presence of a human being is arousing and stimulating in ways that are hard to capture in words. We are affected by a human presence in ways that have not been fully researched but that we all know from our own experience do exist. That dimension of presence (and the stimulation that comes with that presence) is missing on the phone and internet. I have decided that I need to adjust my virtual presence to compensate, even if it moves outside the traditional frame of therapy. I will come back to this topic again, because it is a critical and evolving distinction in the way I am practicing therapy now.

Video platforms, like FaceTime and Zoom, offer a wonderful alternative to meeting in person. In addition to Carol and Bella, I have several other new patients, including a family of four, who started working with me during shelter-in-place. I have only ever met them virtually. With new and ongoing patients alike, video therapy can be lively and provide a space for deep, reflective, and complex work. It is wonderful for us to be able to see each other's facial expressions, body language, dress, and environment.

But there are drawbacks. As with the phone, the heat of in-person meeting is missing. I feel exhausted after a day of Zoom or FaceTime sessions. I know from colleagues that they experience this exhaustion, too. I tend toward stillness and a rigid posture when I'm working on-screen, which gets painful and tiring after several hours. There is a mechanical quality to interacting via screen. Poor sound quality, uneven visual resolution, delays, freezing, and such can make the mechanics of the communication itself a chore. Under normal circumstances, when we are with people, the mechanics of communication are not something we consciously focus on.

There is an intensity of gaze that happens on Zoom, even more than FaceTime, that is markedly different than the quality of gaze that happens in person. It feels like our faces are as close to each other as our face is to our own computer screen. The sensation of that close proximity discourages both patient and therapist from looking away from one another, in order to provide the normal relief from the stimulation of a steady, intense gaze. This continual looking away to break gaze is a normal aspect of human interaction. The relative lack of breaks adds to the tiring effect of working on video platforms.

Neuroscience tells us that more than 90 percent of our thinking is unconscious or subconscious. Which means that in our interpersonal communications, most of what we communicate is expressed and received non-verbally. So much of what is communicated happens in a way that we are only beginning to understand. This mysterious communication source is what many people refer to as a person's energy. I think of this energy as a kind of psychic touch, which can be only partially captured on video.

Like my galvanic skin response to male patients, there are so many in-person variables that are missing over video—the electrical charges between people, the hormones, their small tics. I liked my husband's smell when I met him. Surely that influenced my decision! I have a patient who has to like the shape of a new beau's penis. Her preference is not about size but about its familiarity, so that she can feel at ease allowing the penis inside her.

One of the stranger aspects of working by video is the self-conscious and even surreal aspect of seeing my own image, while wanting and needing to have my eyes on the patient. One of the distinguishing features of psychotherapy used to be that the patient could expect to have the therapist's undivided attention for at least forty-five minutes or whatever the length of the session. To the extent that most of us are eminently distractable, it is especially strange for the distraction to come from seeing my own self. I do not enjoy looking at myself in that small box on FaceTime or the even larger image on Zoom.

Prior to the pandemic, I looked at myself in the morning when I got dressed. I might look again for very brief snippets of time during bathroom breaks throughout the day. Every once in a while, I might scrutinize my image to monitor my weight, my muscle conditioning, my hair, my makeup, my rate of aging, and other aspects of my appearance. For the most part, I am not happy with what I see. My unhappiness is distracting. The moving image of myself in the corner of my screen reminds me of my aging. It used to be that when I wasn't in front of a mirror, I could put my discomfort with my appearance aside and forget about it. Now, I can be momentarily aware of a fleeting bad image and resent that awareness during a session. Or I may glimpse a good view of myself (rare these days) and check back to see if it's still there. On the other side of the relationship, I am not aware of my patients noticing their own images. We have not discussed it, but we should! Most seem absorbed in their process, in their heads and their own drama. Though I have noticed that younger patients will sometimes text during video sessions, which rarely ever happened in person. Kathy once told me that she had straightened her hair during one of our phone sessions.

I never expected, nor wanted, to be faced by all these self-image issues while with a patient. One of the special pleasures of psychotherapy has always been that it gives me an opportunity to forget about myself, to immerse in someone else's inner world. Offering therapy relieves me of myself and feels meditative. As a therapist, I hold multiple narrative and analytical threads in my mind at a time—I am listening for the unconscious, for transference, for factual details of the story, for countertransference (that is, what feelings the patient provokes in me and what that provocation says about the patient and this clinical situation). I am also listening for links to different theoretical lines of inquiry. Does this patient evoke Freudian theory, object relations, trauma and relational theory, or are the difficulties to be found more in the narcissistic line of development, which is a part of all human development? Do the problems stem primarily from Oedipal or pre-Oedipal times? Is this

someone who takes me back to my early work in mother-infant
interaction and who could benefit from the application of some
of those insights?

Later, I ask myself whether the fleeting distraction of seeing my own image is any different from any fleeting thing that
could capture my attention in my office—a plane flying across
the sky or a ladybug on my windowsill. Looking at my image
reminds me that I am on a machine, which, at core, has a more
alienating quality than that charming ladybug or that distant
plane full of imagined passengers.

I've thought a lot about why I don't hide my image, when
that option is available on Zoom. I think the answer is about
symmetry. To hide my own image would create an asymmetry
in my patient's and my modes of being together. In the office,
there is a symmetry in how we are together. We look at each
other, while at the same time maintaining a view of those parts
of ourselves that we can see. Plus, in my office we both have the
same awareness of our own body positions, where we are situated in the room and so on. Eliminating my own image would
create an asymmetry. I would be aware of myself, as if I were in
my office, but alone. The patient would see me and themselves.
As much as I don't love my own image hovering in the corner,
seeing myself is grounding. I am there with my patient!

Fortunately, I am able to push my reactions aside and get
absorbed in the patient's world, just as I would with any other
environmental distraction. I don't know yet what this particular type of visual static is costing me, though undoubtedly it
plays into the exhaustion I've mentioned that I and others experience in working this way. At this point I do not feel that it
interferes with therapy, but the jury is still out.

I meet with the Dean family on Zoom. It's 9:00 a.m. and the first time I am meeting the son. I've worked with this particular couple as they wended their way (with my guidance) through the labyrinthine vagaries of their individual and mutual histories, ultimately alighting on a separation while the father gets sober. Their son is seventeen. I sense that the son feels like a deer in the headlights. We are exploring his feelings about his parents' long and tumultuous marriage. I want and need to make a connection with him, to get a sense of his state of mind, so that I can weave his experience in with those of his parents. I love this work. It energizes and inspires me. It also requires me to be on my toes, emotionally present, my mind working on all cylinders, holding the threads of three individual psychologies and how they interact with one another. I need the social scientist in me to be clicking. I also want to be human and compassionate. This session is the first time the parents have the opportunity to hear their cherished son's experience and painful reactions. His mother starts weeping. She cries for herself and, maybe even more, for her son. We are getting the work done, despite our tenuous, virtual connection.

Virtual Work Takes Its Toll on the Therapist

I am enormously relieved that good work is continuing, despite the transition to virtual platforms. But what about my pleasure? I went into this work to help others and, yes, to serve my own pleasure. I take joy in connecting deeply with another human being and of getting to know the secrets of their minds, in making a difference, in encouraging the conditions for a life well led. While I continue to virtually explore other people's minds,

I have asked myself lately whether I would have gone into this field if I had known that all the work would be by machine. I have never minded the phone, but since the advent of personal computers in the 1990s, I have considered myself lucky to have a job that allowed me to avoid the computer for long stretches of time. I was glad to have work that was about communicating directly with people. The practice of psychotherapy allowed me to be with people in the way I like best—one on one, in the flesh. Devices provide only some of these pleasures. The full experience requires seeing what someone looks like, how they dress, how they move, their physical expressivity, how they come into a room, how they sit or lie down, which seat and where, how they leave, the atmosphere they create, how they look at me, and their reactions to me and my office. As someone who tends toward introversion, psychotherapy has always been an intensely social experience with great meaning.

Another drawback is our literal, technical connection. By early August 2020, the accumulated experiences of poor cell phone reception and stalling FaceTime and Zoom were starting to wear me down. I wonder how my patients feel about the constant interruptions in our therapeutic encounters. *Hang on a minute. You're freezing. Can you hear me now? How is this? Can you speak louder, or wait, I'll adjust the volume?* Finally, we upgraded our internet service at home, and one of my sons showed me how to improve cell reception in the house. What a difference that made. The upgrade eliminated some of the communication strains due to unstable reception, frozen images, and broken-up calls. As reception improved, so did a certain ease of communication. Still, it does not substitute for being in the room with the person.

What will we learn about the effect of these disruptive intrusions into what used to be the sanctuary of the therapy office? Is the therapy space still a haven or just another jangly aspect of the virtual age in which we humans are expected to integrate high and constant levels of noise and fragmentation in our thoughts and sense of cohesiveness? Will we all be driven slowly crazy or become immune to the impingements?

Pre-pandemic, my office projected the serenity that we analysts thought was a necessary precondition for the fruitful introspection of good therapy. I've come to understand that deep work can be done within the context of the aggravating assaults, misfunctioning technology, and less-than-ideal environments. The work requires extra focus and effort, which stretches our internal resources. I used to find the practice of therapy to be meditative. Now, though I still find my work deeply satisfying (and efficacious), it can feel like an exercise in mental gymnastics.

Here's an example. I'm in Martha's Vineyard in a second-floor room that has become a makeshift office I take turns using with my husband. I am on a conference call with the Elfin couple, whom I have been seeing for some time, helping them navigate their marriage after a number of incidents of shoving and slapping. In between these incidents, they have had many enjoyable times in their marriage. Recently they decided to have a trial separation. They are sad and regretful but determined to remain friends, to be good to each other and to continue to enjoy their children and other family members, together. They love each other but they cannot get past their differences, the violence, and the reasons that led to the violence. We are on our conference call working through their ambivalence about starting a separation. She is trying to convince him to find a place to live near their family home, but not *too* near. She still lives in the home with their school-age children. They are surrounded by a community of friends. He is angry because she won't come straight out and say that she wants him to give her space and spend less time in the family home. I try to explain that this argument masks their mutual ambivalence about separating and its implications of a possible divorce. As hard as they try to be nice and respectful, their comments are laced with sadness, anger, fear, and love. The soup of emotions obscures their difficulty letting one another go.

I'm doing this delicate and intense work against the backdrop of the outer margins of Hurricane Isaias. It is black outside. The wind is blowing the office door open and shut. No matter how many things I put in front of the door to hold it shut, nothing works. In the meantime, the connection is faint, I need to press the phone to my ear to hear anything at all. Even then, I'm straining. All the while, I am making the intense effort to sound (and be) relaxed and present, to offer intelligent and useful comments. I pull it off. We have a very productive session. We untangle some knots.

But at what cost? Given how much more taxing the work is, will I be able to see as many patients, or will I have to disappoint some?

My colleagues and I have all found that working remotely, especially on video (versus a clear phone line) is more tiring than practicing therapy in person. At first, I wasn't sure about the energy drain. There were personal energy compensations that came with remote work. I have always found the physical restraint of sitting in the same therapist's chair for hours on end in a small office tiring on long days. I used to feel chained to the same sitting position in an enclosed space. But I did not find the actual practice of therapy to be draining. Now I am both pinned to a single position by a camera, and the work itself demands a different kind of energy and presence.

Will these demands make the work of therapy too different to be appealing? Will I lose patients?

Thirty-five year old Ricardo flat out refused to continue therapy if we couldn't meet in my office. He had been highly engaged in our work for years. He stopped on the spot when shelter-in-place started. He said that he would come back when the pandemic was over. I called him six months into the pandemic to see how he was doing. He asked when I would be back in the office. I told him, when the pandemic was over. He is a high-level professional. He understands my reticence. He sent me a referral. My sense was that his kindness signified a parting gift—sometimes parting ways happens that way. The next time I called him, I left a message, which he did not answer. I imagine the current situation taps into his history of ambiguous loss. His parents, who survived political abuse in an authoritarian regime, were also very self-involved and abandoned him emotionally. Virtual therapy felt too distant for him. Then, just as the vaccines were rolling out, Ricardo came back, this time virtually. We are all constantly reassessing what changes we can accept.

Privacy can also be a challenge. I've met with Frank twice a week in person for years. He says he might cut back to once a week. While his emotional state is sensitive, reactive and often volatile, there is an overall consistency and stability in his lifestyle and a steady commitment to his obligations in life. I don't think he is ready now, yet he may be preparing himself for cutting back in the future, when he feels a stronger sense of internal quiescence. During our phone sessions, he mentions in passing that he can't talk as freely to me about his wife, because she is in the house. When I ask him directly, he agrees that his lack of privacy might be a factor in cutting back, rather than really being ready. Several months later, this possibility has been placed on the back burner, as Frank traverses a period of intense grieving over the death of both parents and his children's growing independence. I hear the grief for his youth and younger adulthood hovering in the background.

Another young patient stopped during the pandemic, because her parents could not continue to pay. Her father's business has declined significantly during the pandemic.

Pre-pandemic, I took so much of the frame for granted. Now every element seems to be in play, up to and including the way we approach the work itself.

The New Landscape of Self-Disclosure

As you will have no doubt noticed by now, I keep referring to the new ways I am addressing my patients' issues. These times and new platforms call for a refinement and a refresh of therapeutic techniques. As anyone who has been in talk therapy or specifically psychoanalytic therapy has undoubtedly noticed, therapists tend not to reveal much, if any, personal information about themselves to patients. This has been a basic tenet, the *sine qua non* since its inception. There is good reason for this standard. The idea, as conceived of by Freud, is that analytic therapists should be blank screens onto which patients can project their wishes, fears, and, in a more contemporary view, their personalities.

Over the last few decades, the standard has softened some. For good theoretical and clinical reasons, some ease has developed around the practice. Most of us agree that there are times and conditions when we might share something personal. We recognize that the therapy experience is intersubjective. We cannot act as if the only subjectivity in the room is the patient. There are two subjective presences. Still, the standard of offering a neutral presence persists for good reason. We don't want to make the therapy about ourselves or to interfere with the patient's projection of their own self into the therapeutic space. We want to see what emerges from the patient without nudging, influencing, or guiding them in any way. Since Freud, analysts have agreed, for the most part, that an occasional self-disclosure by the therapist not only is *not* harmful but can be helpful.

We also know that patients know that we are not blank screens. We understand that patients know way more about us, simply from their observations, than is openly acknowledged by both of us. Our patients are aware that we are human beings, thus, innately, irreducibly subjective. This is one of those dualities that exist in life, as in psychoanalytic therapy. We conspire to preserve the blank-screen idea, an important and useful standard, even as we recognize each other's humanity. We are at once subjective and neutral. We are relating as one human to the next. Yet maintaining the ideal of the therapist as a neutral canvas enables us to better elicit our patients' fantasies and inner life imaginings. This is our shared, implicit complicity. The therapist retains their authority without sliding into an authoritarian posture, which fails to recognize intersubjectivity.

What are self-disclosures anyway? Disclosures are anything the therapist reveals about herself to the patient. This could range from giving information like where you are going for vacation to revealing a political sentiment or sharing a feeling you have about the patient (historically a taboo). It's not that we therapists pretend that we don't have feelings for our patients. Quite the contrary. It's just that when feelings occur, we try to understand what they are telling us about our patient. Am I sleepy when usually I'm alert? Am I feeling angry and taken advantage of by a last-minute change in the session time (or many sessions), or a low fee that I haven't renegotiated? My job, when I encounter strong feelings, is to ask myself what about the patient's behavior or words is eliciting the feelings, to examine my feelings to make sure they aren't my own baggage, which I might be wrongly attributing to the patient. For this reason, it is extremely important that therapists have plenty of therapy, so that they know themselves as well as they can—even (and especially) the parts of themselves that are difficult to confront.

The radical changes that the pandemic wrought in both society and how we practice therapy has necessitated more disclosures, in large part because of the shift to that greater sense of partnership in the work that I've mentioned—a sense that we are all experiencing the same disaster at the same time, and that the virtual aspect of the work requires greater efforts to humanize it.

During shelter-in-place, I shared with patients in a more partner-like way, sometimes chatting about little details of our shared situation, the sirens, the vagaries of working from home, pandemic facts and safety measures, the destabilizing experi-

ence of having to reorganize my billing system, supply short-
ages, etc. In the first few virtual sessions with a patient, I
painted the room, letting them know where I was, if I was sitting
or walking. I, in turn, listened for details of the patient's new
lifestyle arrangements as a way to *paint* the space of their life.

Linda mentions the problem of her gray hair roots, and I tell
her that I use Revlon ColorSilk at home to cover my gray roots.

Frank and I discuss the differences between ordinary cognitive decline versus the dementia that his parents are experiencing in their later life. With this same patient, and select
others, I do not hide my political sentiments, though early in
the pandemic I tried not to share my politics and restrained
myself to a murmur here and there. Beginning in late Septem-
ber 2020, I start to talk politics with him. He has always taken
politics extremely seriously and is beside himself over the political situation. On my side, I now regard the political situation
as akin to the weather. A rainstorm or hurricane is a fact that
cannot be denied and affects most people. There is a real insan-
ity that has nothing to do with political philosophy and that
cannot be denied without manipulating our shared reality. So,
I talk politics and even share some of my views, as long as they
are neutral observations of fact, such as comments about the
erosion of our democracy that are unrelated to my political party
of choice.

Throughout the fall of 2020, politics was a particularly difficult topic to avoid, because of the compounding effect of the
political situation on the pandemic. When I think about the
situation therapeutically, a government is like a set of parents.
In order to feel secure, we need to have confidence in our parents
and their leadership. The same goes for being a citizen in a

country, especially during a crisis like the pandemic. Part of my job as a therapist is to keep in mind the patient's sense of reality and to shine a light on their behavior and reactions. That sense of reality was more shared than ever before.

In addition to Frank, I had political discussions with a couple of other patients. Throughout my career, I have listened to patients discuss politics. Pre-pandemic, I discussed patients' political views in terms of the personal meaning in the context of the individual patient's life. During the pandemic (and all else), there has been a huge uptick in the number of patients discussing politics and the length of time they spend discussing it. Patients' (really, all of our) moods are more likely to be affected by politics. Several of my patients are passionate in their feelings and feel profoundly, personally affected by this government.

In response to the reality of this period of political turmoil, I allowed myself to join in the political discussion without necessarily interpreting a patient's views as a psychological issue. Sometimes there is nothing to interpret. I joined in, because I thought that Trump and his administration were not about politics. They were about a gross and destructive distortion of character. They were about a radical violation of the norms of human behavior and governmental leadership. I decided that to treat patients' distress over the previous administration as an idiosyncratic reaction to politics as usual would be to gaslight my patients. I had to validate their view of reality. If there was a tornado or an earthquake, wouldn't I discuss that as a real event and examine my patients' emotional reaction to it within the bounds of normalcy? Wouldn't it have been disingenuous if I had acted as if I, unlike my patients, was not affected by the Trump administration's actions? As if I were somehow living outside the context? In this, I was acting as a partner to my patients. We were both suffering the depredations of the pandemic. We were both living with a surreal political situation.

Of course, where it seemed relevant, meaningful, and appropriate, I still worked to discern my patients' reactions within the framework of their history and personality. But for the three particular patients who felt so passionate, the individual psychic explanation was secondary. Linda spends a session complaining about President Trump and his Republican supporters. She is upset. Her responses reflect realistic concerns about his behavior and policies. They are related to the facts of what is going on. In spite of her distress over the current administration, her mood is calm and confident. Early in our session, I'm thinking about what the political situation means to her in a personal way. Then I realize that Linda is having a perfectly rational response to a set of facts about the Trump administration. I allow myself to get into a political discussion with her. While this is, obviously, something I rarely do with patients, I assess that Linda is having a real reaction to a real situation, not a psychic distortion of reality. I say, "We are dependent on a leader who is unrecognizable as a human being. He's like a different species of human being." I affirm that she sees Trump's political supporters as enablers who know better. I affirm her and our mutual reality. She is reassured.

At the same time, I never lose track of the fact that I am practicing therapy and that where I can, I should and will always tie a patient's responses back to the personal meaning the situation has for the individual patient.

A disclosure can be a way of greasing the skids. I've noticed that some patients need more prompts in virtual sessions to keep associating, Like the Mahler baby checking back with the care-giver, they are wondering where I am. Before the pandemic, if I did a phone session, patients could imagine me in my office, even when they weren't there. Now my patients literally cannot place me in their mind's eye. Some people can adjust. They feel secure that I am there. They are okay imagining my surround-ings. Others cannot place me so easily. The Revlon ColorSilk comment was my response to sensing that Linda was feeling a blankness about me, a worry that she had lost me. Linda often feels highly self-conscious and undeserving of the time we spend discussing her. The ColorSilk comment was my way of bridg-ing the divide, reaching out to her in a human way. As if to say, "I, too, suffer from gray hair roots and the loss of my hair salon. Imagine me as I am." This is authenticity. This is what mirror-ing can look like when I can't offer her the mirror of my live, in-person face, as I do when we are together in my office.

Without disclosures, I sense that some of my patients are panicked that I am disappearing and our connection is fraying. With those patients I must work really hard to bridge the gap. In this new paradigm, I need to figure out ways to let my pa-tients know that I understand their feelings around the loss of my presence and give them something to hang on to between sessions. While some can benefit simply by discussing this phe-nomenon of loss, others need something more literal, a self-disclosure, to tide them over until they feel more secure.

Therapist self-disclosures have always been one of the trick-iest, most challenging types of responses to determine if, when, and how to use. There is a natural human pull toward bringing oneself into the conversation. As therapists we are so trained to not discuss ourselves with a patient that we experience a double strain. We are tempted to refer to ourselves, while simultaneously feeling like it is a sin. A good therapist is a listener more than a sharer. Our hiding spot behind the couch, so to speak, feels comfortable and safe. The challenging part is to make an in-the-moment decision during a therapeutic encounter. It can be hard to decide what's appropriate, especially in the real time of a psychotherapy session. My work is to stay present for the patient and not disappear into my own head. Yet I also have to listen to my intuition when it tells me to share something about myself. In that split second, we therapists must ask ourselves: Is this useful to the patient? To what end are we sharing this piece of personal information? What good will it do the patient, or is its only purpose to gratify ourselves?

Though I am talking more these days, there are times, as I strain to listen for the underlying meaning in the patient's process, that I actively defend myself against my impulse to talk. As much as the impositions of the pandemic require more self-disclosure, I do not always make the right choice. I catch myself making a self-disclosure, asking a question, or making an interpretation prompted by my own anxiety, which generates a miscalculation in my timing and the need of the patient.

When I first meet Bella on Zoom, she speaks haltingly, as if in pain. It is difficult for her to start. In our communications prior to meeting in our first session, she had impressed me as an in-charge, commanding person, with not a hint of the insecurity I see on that first day. At the beginning of the session, Bella tells me that she went to my high school alma mater. She says she's glad that like her, I am female and have an office in her building. I am surprised that she doesn't say anything about the alma mater part, since the person who referred her to me knows that we went to the same school. I tell her this. Instead, I should have said, "You wish I could understand and be there for you, but you are not sure you can trust that I can." That response would have furthered the work of therapy, rather than simply revealing my similar origins. She would have learned something about herself and seen that indeed I did understand something deep about her.

Later, I analyzed my compulsion to self-disclosure with Bella. Anxiety is contagious. I recognized that I had caught her anxiety. As a result of her fear that people she depends upon will use her vulnerability for their own means, dishonor her and let her down, she herself has an unreliable quality about her. That made me anxious. It awakened my need to find a quick bridge instead of engaging in the harder, slower work of making an interpretation that would lead to insight and trust.

I'm listening to an accomplished, thoughtful patient struggle with a sense of meaninglessness and powerlessness. I feel like there is nothing for me to say. She is doing the work we want our patients to do. She is facing a kind of pain she has avoided until recently. Up until about two years ago, she actively avoided feelings of depression, hopelessness, powerlessness, and pessimism. She has always been a can-do, look-on-the-bright-side problem solver, a coping strategy she developed in the aftermath of her mother's sudden death when she was a preteen, left alone with her father and two siblings. She is a jokester and often resorts to humor when dark or negative feelings loom.

Now, Emma is taking on those hard feelings and grappling with what her life means. I realize that I have some of these same feelings nipping at the door of my consciousness and they are getting in the way of my usual interpretive presence. Instead of saying, "You are struggling to find meaning in your life," I break my long silence with an overly complicated interpretation of what she's been talking about. I'm caught up in my own morass, questioning my own meaning and power.

Another day Emma is exploring and expanding on her views about the political and social scene, the current administration and how history ties into the present and future. I feel engaged in the subject matter and in Emma's thinking process. I recognize that part of what she needs out of the session is a companion in her thinking process and the space to develop her ideas. I wonder whether she needs permission to develop this side of herself. In a moment of enthusiasm, I suggest that Emma might enjoy the recent podcast put out by Sam Harris. Harris, a neuroscientist and philosopher, had given a brilliant analysis of President Trump, his psychology, his goals, what needs he satisfied in the American public, and the challenge of defeating him.

I'm not 100 percent sure that the recommendation is the right thing. In the little time I have to consider my decision, I mentally rule in the direction of my hunch that Emma is looking for a partner in her reflections. I know that psychoanalytic technique would counsel abstinence, but I rationalize my decision on the basis that our Zoom meetings create a need for more concrete outreach.

Emma's reaction catches me off guard. She dutifully starts to write down my suggestion. Then she starts talking about having a reading and writing learning disorder. These already cause her to avoid the stack of reading piling up on her bedside. Instead of sounding delighted by my recommendation, she sounds politely burdened and vaguely anxious. I realize my

mistake. Emma wants me to listen, to be an appreciative sounding board and possibly even to admire her mind. She does not
need my participation in her out-loud thinking process. She
enjoys the workings of her own mind. Through my attentive
listening, punctuated with my occasional efforts at making
sense of her perambulations, she gains permission, inspira-
tion, and insight for using and understanding her own mind in
this way. I pivot and inquire about her feeling burdened by my
assignment. This bears fruit, opening up an exploration of her
feelings about reading versus talking.

I attribute this misstep to meeting exclusively remotely. I am
still working on my timing, this new choreography of psychotherapy, when to intervene and say something and when to stay
silent, when to ask a question, make a self-disclosure, and when
not. The dance is not as intuitive as it was face-to-face in the
office. I am developing new skills as the pandemic wears on, set-
tling into this new therapy landscape.

I have always had multiple threads running through my head
during sessions, a series of scrolling news banners of thoughts
and reactions while the patient is talking. There's the news banner of what the patient is saying. The news banner of my own
idiosyncratic thoughts and possible responses, which might not
be the right thing to say to the patient. What I'm observing and
theorizing. Finally, there is what I tell myself is the appropriate
response for the circumstance. When Emma was discussing her
worldviews, my scrolling news banner suggested I offer my
views. At other times, my banner displays my mental notes,
reactions, and theories about the patient. Whether to share
these thoughts, in what form, and why—these are the critical
questions. The ultimate question is whether my input will help

the patient. Occasionally now, it's harder to know if I'm just trying to satisfy my own need or curiosity as a way to combat the flatness or more softly etched cues that can set into virtual interactions.

Despite the missteps, I am getting my self-disclosures mostly right.

Sylvia is talking about how her husband doesn't see what needs to be done around the house. I nod in agreement and allow a soft chuckle to escape, obliquely revealing that I am personally familiar with such phenomena. Sylvia's normal affect is laconic. In this case, she allows herself a slight laugh in response, and her tone is warm and appreciative. Signs that Sylvia is relaxing into the work of therapy.

I use the same tone of complicit understanding with Beth. She's talking about the challenge of being pregnant while having a toddler—how hard it is, how tiring, how the work is endless. I let her know that I remember those utterly exhausting days, when sometimes I didn't know how I would get through them. How I couldn't understand why nature set things up the way it did. How I felt, like Beth, that no one was there to help me through.

Beth not only appreciates my words, but she opens up and free-associates more, an encouraging sign that the therapy process is going well. A well-timed interpretation that sparks more associations, more memories, and more material is an important craft in our work. Beth talks more about her repressed upbringing, the shame she feels every time her life is not matching up to a glossy women's magazine ideal and the guilt she experiences because she needs engagement and stimulation other than childcare. She tells me that she is ashamed of her occasional bouts of boredom and exhaustion caring for her toddler. I support her new, disclosive freedom with my own minor self-disclosures.

Humor is another aid we might naturally reach for to liven the environment. Yet even the therapist's use of humor can serve as a kind of self-disclosure, so I need to stay alert to how I use it.

In our session, Ellie mentions yet again that she thinks that I know everything. She says she knows this can't be true, but she catches herself feeling that way. She tells me about how she is grappling with the irritation this causes her, because it makes her feel an uneasy sense of dependence on me. As she looks for the words to finish the thought, I say, "I'm not God." She laughs and says, "Unless something has changed in the last two weeks." I say, "Weelll . . . I have something to tell you . . ." We both laugh.

I might have told this joke pre-pandemic, but I'm inspired by the new looseness I've allowed myself since the pandemic came on the scene. This looser quality in our interaction springs from the reality that we are all in this together. My joke responds to what I sense of Ellie's anxiety in the moment. As her anxiety mounts, I naturally slip into the humor she responds so well to.

Ellie knows I'm not God. I know she knows. My joke reveals, surreptitiously, that a little part of me might enjoy being God for Ellie and that a part of Ellie might want me to be godlike.

In every child's development, there is a need to believe that her parents are omnipotent. In times of vulnerability, the child *borrows* from this perception of the parent's power to shore up their own security. This same type of dynamic often comes up in therapy between therapist and patient. It can signal areas of the patient's development that were lacking or unfinished. Ellie and I have spoken a lot about her frustration, anger, and sadness that her dad was not more of a success in life. Ellie would have liked to be able to look up to her father more, to view him as a more powerful figure. Ellie's uneasy dependence on me stems from the fleeting ways in which I stand in, at times, for her wished-for father. My revealing humor eases Ellie.

Use of the Self and Personal Theories

The pandemic made me realize that one of the things that originally attracted me to psychoanalysis and psychoanalytic therapy is the implicit artistry of the work. The ways in which an analytic therapist uses their most personal self (something that artists do) in service of another. For me, the analyst's *self* includes the entire spectrum of the analyst's thoughts, feelings, character, and experience—all the things that make up intuition. Ironically, at the most conscious level, I was drawn to the work first by the scientific rigor of the psychoanalytic method as a way to understand human behavior. When I first started learning about psychoanalysis in twelfth grade, I loved diving into the psychoanalytic theories. I didn't want to be paid to be someone's friend. I wanted the scientific rigor and legitimacy of being a trained professional. I was forged in the discipline of ballet and academically demanding schools. I still have an enormous appreciation for the invaluable insights gained by the scientific methodology, as a structure to understand human character and pathology. Yet, alongside the rigor, I have allowed my love for the artistry of the work back into my consciousness. Just as in

ballet, it is the harmony of rigor and artistry that attracts me to
therapy. The creative work of therapy was always something that
I sensed was present but could not quite put into words, or even
thoroughly admit existed. Only recently has it become less professionally threatening for a therapist to admit to the artistry of
our field.

Take, for example, the emotions a patient elicits in me. These
kinds of feelings are called countertransference. Under Freud,
one's countertransference was something to be aware of and
understood, but then avoided or even done away with, because
it could be harmful to the patient. Yet I've always thought it was
fascinating to try to figure out what the emotions elicited by a
patient were trying to tell me. When I first started seeing
patients in graduate school, I delighted in trying to decipher my
countertransference and would dig into the information my
feelings were giving me when patients caused a strong or un-
usual reaction in me.

Several decades after Freud's death, analysts have started to
explore the importance of the feelings our patients provoke in
us in new ways. We have finally and formally acknowledged
what we always knew privately: not only can we not avoid having feelings, they contain a gold mine of information about the
patient. Not only should we not avoid them, but an essential
part of our work is to pay close attention to what these countertransference feelings are telling us.

In his writing about the use and understanding of the analyst's reverie, Thomas Ogden, an analyst, has augmented our
countertransference tool kit. Reverie refers to the points where
the analyst's thoughts wander, even as they are simultaneously
listening to the patient. Reverie may also include the period of

anticipating a patient's arrival or right after their departure. To be able to use these tools effectively requires extensive analytic training, broad clinical experience, knowledge of oneself, and discipline. As I've mentioned before, we need to keep asking ourselves, "What does this mean to me? What does this mean about the patient?" A therapist has to be able to reflect on their reverie openly and creatively—this is an aspect of what I call the People Art of psychotherapy.

Reverie and countertransference and the use of intuition are examples of how the analyst uses her very *self* in the work of analysis. It is the therapist's use of the self that makes her an artist. Her access to her unconscious self is what promotes true therapeutic creativity. Freud described such unconscious communications as one person's telephone receiver turned toward another's receiver in order to *hear* an unconscious communication. Psychoanalytic training is all about *listening with the third ear*, as Theodor Reik called it in his book of the same title. That is, listening for the unconscious thoughts and feelings and for the hidden meaning encoded in conscious thoughts, which are revealed in the patient's everyday speech.

I imagine Freud, and his lineage of great analysts, listening with their third ears, hearing new things and developing their theories to fit their patients. In this book, I am describing my own sharpened hearing as I listen with the third ear to what the pandemic means in my patients' lives. But I'm also *listening* for how the pandemic has been a crystallizing event in the evolution of psychotherapeutic theory and practice, so that our work can be responsive to how people actually live and think and feel.

In addition to the theories we learn, we therapists each have our own personal ideas about the practice of therapy. Ideas that we conceived of on our own and that did not come from formal training or education. This is a startling but unsurprising idea. Startling, because we study and rely on an enormous volume of formal, recorded theory and technique, handed down over the years, from teachers to students, and copious publications. Unsurprising, because we each know, at some level, that we bring personal theories to our work.

Personal theories are a sophisticated idea that goes beyond the formal, established theories that we therapists spend years thinking about—how to use them, which to use, when and how to apply them to actual clinical situations. Personal theories capture an essence about how each of us approaches our work—we all have unspoken assumptions about the practice of therapy. Most are unconscious and even difficult to identify and put into words.

Most of us developed at least some, if not most, of our personal theories long before our formal training. They are not easy to conceptualize, because most, if not all, of them are either completely unconscious or at least subconscious. They are so seamlessly melded with the recognized, formal theory and technique that we've learned that it is difficult to tease apart which is which. They are also difficult to discern separately, because they are bound up with what attracted us to the field in the first place, what resonated with our own beliefs before we joined the field. The work of psychoanalysis provided a form and function for our preexisting proclivities. Not a lot has been written about analysts' use of personal theories. I first read that personal theories existed several years before the pandemic struck, in the work of Joseph Sandler, a psychoanalytic writer, and later in the beautiful writing of Michael Parsons, another psychoanalyst.

Captivated by the idea, I went on to read more of the work of a highly regarded teacher and figure in our field, Lew Aron and his colleague Galit Atlas, both of whom dealt with a similar idea. I have been refining my thinking about my personal theories ever since, considering how they may complement and enhance the traditional features of the work of psychotherapy.

One of my personal theories, which preexisted anything I learned about psychoanalysis, was that we can and should use our feeling about another person to understand that person. A former analyst of mine used to say, "Analysts are born, not made." I have always felt that first I was an analyst. Later I got trained. I first used my intuition, personal reactions, and, of course, my intellect (!) as a way to understand what my parents and brothers needed. In fact, to my detriment, I used empathy to understand and take care of them, rather than to understand what I needed. That part took training.

Four months into the pandemic and shelter-in-place restrictions, I realized, even more keenly than before, that much of what drew me to psychoanalysis in the first place, and that has become one of the pillars of the work for me, is this personal artistry of interpreting not only the patient's psychology but also my own and how these two angles intersect to help me understand my patient. Though I've mentioned the importance of our eyes and other sensors, and they cannot be underestimated, the analyst's ear is still her main therapeutic instrument, attuned to interpret through the filter of her personal theories, while always drawing on the theories from her formal training.

Another of my personal theories is that warmth (aka analytic love) greatly enhances the chance of cure in psychotherapy.

There are different definitions of what qualifies as a *cure* in psychoanalysis. Without getting deeply into theory, I define cure as the patient feeling substantially better. That can mean different things depending on the patient. The patient feels more sense of choice in how they lead their lives, gets more satisfaction, makes peace with a long-standing situation, changes their situation, deals better with reality, distorts less in how they perceive people, interactions, and events. They get better at coping with life.

My proclivity toward listening with sincere care and interest and to invest in the well-being of the other has encouraged people to want to talk to me and confide in me from an early age. They are the same traits that made my family members look to me to prioritize them and to cater to their needs. Typical of many therapists, until I was trained, this was my MO with far too many people in my life. This orientation toward care, combined with my curiosity about others and the goings-on in their minds, was a large part of what led me to the profession. But in my training, I learned to be more selective in my expressions of care and curiosity and not to give it out indiscriminately. I developed a sense of choice about my orientation and decided to direct it toward patients and others of my choosing. Of course, I've always understood that the analytic method and the insights gained are not etched in stone. Freud himself believed that analytic love had to be part of the cure. Unfortunately, professionalism and the scientific rigor of the psychoanalytic method led a generation of American analysts to take his ideas of *neutrality*, *abstinence* and *anonymity* and carry them forward to create a kind of cold and unnatural behavior in some therapists. That is not what Freud meant, and this misunderstanding had an enormous impact on our practice. All that Freud meant by neutrality was that the analyst should not favor the patient's id, ego, or superego.

These concepts (neutrality, abstinence, anonymity, id, ego, and superego) get tossed around a lot, so it's worth taking another brief psycho-ed pause to clarify our shared understanding. Let's start with the id, that reservoir of primitive affects, our emotions, drives, wishes, desires, and fears. A child caught eating chocolate ice cream is chastised by the parent. The parent thinks they are speaking in neutral tones. The child sees a huge, menacing figure threatening her sense of emotional or possibly physical safety. Here are some other classic id desires: I want to sleep with my mother, kill my father, or sleep with the woman in my aisle at the supermarket, even though I'm married. Our superego is the conscience that regulates our id and sets our ideal standards, which may or may not be realistic. The ego is our coping capacity, our life skills and our repertoire of defenses and protections against unwanted, unrecognized, or potentially disruptive wishes, fears, and feelings.

The analyst is looking at how integrated the id and superego are. Ideally, a patient manages their superego so it doesn't crush them with its demands and high standards, and simultaneously manages the id's desires so they are satisfied enough by life, but not running amok. The ego helps them find this balance. The analyst is looking at their patients' interpersonal skills, their life skills, their coping skills. The analyst's role is to help the patient understand herself and figure out what's good for her. Help her find a healthier balance between the id, superego, and ego.

For example, I have a patient who is in a toxic marriage, which is deeply unsatisfying. She and her husband have established parallel lives and can no longer bridge the distance that exists between them. She has discussed the idea of having an affair or whether she should leave her husband. As her therapist, it is not my role to favor one or the other of those decisions. In her case, my patient's superego is excessively harsh and punishes her for the least thought she has about another man. Maybe an affair, or at least its consideration, would help balance her id and superego. I would certainly never encourage such a decision. Simply considering an affair, without having one *and* without punishing herself for the thought, would allow for a more comfortable relationship with herself, her needs, and her decisions in life. My goal is to surface the reasons why she deprives herself and how she might find better balance. That is the practice of neutrality.

Abstinence is therapy's term of art to describe the ways in which a therapist should abstain from talking, unless they have something important to say. Traditionally, every time a psychoanalytic therapist is moved to ask a question, she must ask herself, am I asking out of analytic or personal curiosity, or some other reason which may not serve the therapy? *Anonymity* is therapy's term of art to describe the analytic practice of not making self-disclosures. Both of these elements of analytic technique are good disciplines and have their place, but there is a danger, too, that these theories have ossified, that they feel cold or stultifying to our patients.

As I was figuring out how to bring more of my true self (who listens with care and warmth) into my work, because I believed it could increase the efficacy of my work as a therapist, I started seeing a new analyst myself. Vince was highly trained in traditional psychoanalysis, including his respect for the notions of neutrality, anonymity, abstinence. He was serious about professional practice and knowledgeable about theory and technique. He was very senior and had been in practice for decades. He had developed his own style and philosophy of practice. Yet he did not hide his interest in me as a person, that he cared about me and wanted to help me feel better. That combination made an enormous difference in the outcome of my work with him. It was only after my work with Vince that I was finally ready to stop therapy. I felt able to essentially be my own analyst, which, according to some theories, is the hallmark of being ready for *termination*, as we analysts call the patient's readiness to stop therapy.

Vince found ways to show warmth without crossing any ethical or therapeutic boundaries. He did not act like my friend, nor did he say, "I love you." Here is what he did do. First, he spoke to me in a way that no other therapist had ever spoken to me. His style of speech was natural, as if he were speaking to a friend, yet more thoughtful than if he were speaking socially. He would lean forward and look at me intently. Sometimes his searching looks even annoyed me, but that was my issue. Mostly, his looks signaled to me how hard he was working to understand the meaning of what I was saying. At times, he would use a beseeching tone of voice, which also annoyed me, but, again, which also told me how much he cared. He so wanted to me to understand, because it was important for me. His whole emotional tone told me that he liked me and enjoyed who I am. He recognized my strengths, validated my observations and experiences, often with feeling and emphasis.

We could argue and both be mad. Yet his anger didn't feel threatening. Well, maybe a tiny bit. All anger is at minimum somewhat threatening to all people. His anger made me mad right back at him. I was trying to make myself understood in those moments. He never retaliated and would often come back, sometimes in a phone message after I left the session, to let me know that he had reflected on what I said and he thought he could understand what I was trying to communicate to him. When he felt that nothing else would make the point better, he told me things about himself that he thought would convince me of a point he was trying to make.

As with his looks and tone and anger, I did not always like his self-disclosures, nor did they necessarily change my view. For instance, he once told me, in an effort to convince me that aging was not the end of my feminine appeal, that he still found his partner sexy. He and his wife are a generation older than me. While I was not convinced by this particular piece of information, the idea that he shared it with me told me that he trusted me and cared enough about helping me that he was willing to expose himself in order to get through to me. In my younger years, I would not have had the capacity to handle this sort of revelation. But Vince judged, correctly, that my personal evolution was far enough along that I could absorb the information without disruption and possibly even benefit.

Though I have emphasized Vince's unique warmth and self-disclosures, in fact, he spoke very sparingly about himself. He did not ask me questions only to satisfy his curiosity. He used his curiosity to benefit my welfare. He did not take sides between my wishes, fears, and conscience. He did occasionally hold up what he felt was an important mirror to reality, when he felt I was unnecessarily hard on myself. In my early years of going to therapy, with other therapists, I occasionally chatted with my therapist and asked questions. I only needed to get shut down a few times to learn to talk only about myself in therapy. Vince's warmth signaled a caring intention. This intent was one of the potent (and new, to me) ingredients he brought to his work, and which enabled me to change.

In addition to his authenticity and vitality, of course, Vince had all the traditional analytic insights, based in verbal interpretation and theory.

Armed with Vince's love and interest, I unloaded. I told him things in a fresh, unselfconscious manner, unconstrained by guilt and shame. He saw as much of the real me as I have ever shown to anyone, except perhaps in a long, committed romantic relationship. Unless we are psychotic, we all hold back a sliver of ourselves in the presence of another. In sessions with Vince, I was passionate and intense, strong emotions I often hold back, because I fear that my intensity will be unwanted.

Outside the therapy room, my confidence grew. I began to appreciate myself more—who I was, my wishes, desires, dislikes, and style of behavior. I began to like more parts of myself, even my intensity and passion—aspects of myself that I hadn't liked since earlier periods of my life, when I was in settings where a cool affect was the norm. I also learned to like my quiet introversion, which eventually makes me feel like I don't fit into any given group. I'm not naturally assertive in the way that is required to be heard. I get tired talking in a group for an extended period. I can be very shy in one circumstance and extroverted in another. People who see me in one mode of behavior get a mistaken impression of who I am. I am both. As a result of my work with Vince, I began to embrace all my disparate and seemingly contradictory traits and those ways in which some of my sensibilities differ from others, causing me to feel *other*. I accepted my tendency to dislike crime, law, and espionage movies and TV. I accepted my preference for slow-moving psychological dramas. I don't like board games. I need to exercise intensely every day. I simultaneously embrace fashion *and* I engage in deep thought and sensitive analysis of myself and others. I do not shy away from the kinds of challenging conversations that are so often veiled in euphemisms. I am *extremely* curious about others and notice the tiniest details about them. With that comes a drive to help. I wonder whether I am weird in my intense focus on the details of the other person, including their inner life. I have limited patience for non-genuine connections with others, but delight in razor sharp, irreverent humor. Brief and fleeting, even shallow connections are enjoyable as long as they are not fake. I don't like to speak on the phone or video for more than short bursts, even during the pandemic, unless it's a patient session.

Such self-acceptance and dare I say even liking myself (which is different from self-love and harder to achieve) has benefited me in ways I never could have guessed. I may be a therapist, but like everyone else, I don't necessarily see how things are standing in my way. I had epiphanies that revealed issues I wasn't aware of. I forgive myself more easily for the petty misdemeanors of everyday life. I don't get especially worried if I make someone mad (I am still working on that one with my children). I have confidence that they will get over their anger, and even if they don't, we will both survive. This self-acceptance is what analysts call *softening* a harsh superego (recall that's our conscience and our self-punishing mechanism). I am better at giving myself permission to pursue my interests and desires, even if it means disappointing others. When I do sacrifice my own needs, I do it with a sense of choice rather than compulsion. The increased solitude of these times has given me time to walk deeper into this self-knowledge and further develop my compassionate friendship with myself.

One more thing Vince once said: "Well, there aren't that many really good people in the world." With this sweeping generalization about the world, Vince gave me his subjective view of reality (derived, to be sure, from his observations of nearly eight decades of living and therapy practice). He philosophized, which is un-therapy-like, according to formal technique. Yet most therapists will do it at least occasionally. His comment helped me distinguish my personal perceptions that I was doing something wrong to elicit someone's bad treatment, from a possible greater truth about that person's character that was outside myself. I don't presume to know all the qualities that constitute a good person. Still, I was able to understand that I was not doing something wrong to invite (or deserve) bad behavior. Beyond my personal therapeutic situation in that session, hearing Vince allow himself to give his opinion in turn gave me further permission to occasionally make a statement like that instead of only exploring the patient's perceptions.

Behind all these changes is Vince, the work we did together, how he let me know that it's okay to be me and more than anything, that it is okay to be simply human. I think of Vince now— when I normalize, generalize or philosophize; when I bring my *self* into the work; when I'm human with my patients.

Which brings me back to the pandemic and the way it focused me on my own theories about psychotherapy. There is no literature about how to practice under such crisis conditions.

I was compelled to dig into my internal resources in ways I had not done since childhood and with more awareness than when I was a very young person. My work with Vince gave me new fortitude to trust my own mind, my intuition, and the urgently felt need to be creative.

For many years, Vince stretched the rules of abstinence and anonymity. He shared things about himself. He was looser and more open than any other analyst I had ever met. He started the process of loosening me up. The pandemic pulled on those same threads to allow even more expansiveness. Though Vince made few self-disclosures, they were notable and important. Not for their content, but because he signaled that, in service of my well-being, he wasn't rigidly sticking to the rules. He was human. He even permitted himself a few judicious analyses of important people in my life, sometimes risking accuracy (though he was pretty much always right about these). His methods (and their efficacy) liberated me to be more creative. So I have permitted myself to go into uncharted waters, as the world itself has entered the new territory of a pandemic in the modern age.

The warmth I use creates a bridge with patients. Especially since the pandemic and the move to all remote work, my tone is more welcoming. I literally say *yes* more often and nod my head more frequently, to signal that I am with the patient. On occasion now, I offer straight-up reassurance. As a therapist, I cannot explore and understand my patient's dilemma if I am too reassuring. Reassurance can shut down a topic. I need to find the balance that can help to repair the bridge that has been weakened by our inability to be in a room together.

Ken speaks painfully about longing for his father's elusive and limited supply of love, approval and admiration. He talks about how he envies his sister, the child who always seemed to get his father's love. He even talks about envying his mother for receiving some of his father's love, too. I help Ken make the connection between his wishes for his father's love, his envy of his sister and mother. The way these dynamics designed a template for his love life, in which he always pursues unavailable men who devalue him. As we wade into this sensitive territory, making connections between these three painful dynamics, Ken blurts out, "Will you stick with me through this journey?"

A lot of traditional theories counsel the therapist to answer in a neutral tone and non-committal answer, or even with a question about the meaning of Ken's question. I do not want to sidestep his anguish. His question shows that he understands the importance of the subject matter we are diving into and the courage it will take him to go deeper. I reassure him that I will accompany his inward journey. I tell him that I appreciate how brave and difficult the journey is for him.

As I have gained experience, I have gotten more in touch with how I use personal theories and how I understand what they are. As we navigate the work of therapy within these pandemic circumstances, it becomes increasingly necessary to fall back on our own ideas.

I've already mentioned several of my personal theories—the importance of the self and the restrained integration of natural warmth; here is a more robust sample.

1. First, be human, be curious, be interested. Ask questions when important. My curiosity facilitates the patient's desire to talk and share and to feel safe in the knowledge that I want to hear them.

2. Think developmentally. What made people the way they are? What happened in their development to influence them? What level of development does their behavior correspond to now?

3. Empathy is not a technique. It must be part of you. Fortunately, most of us possess the quality of empathy, though we may need to develop and hone it.

4. Prioritize the flow. One of the most important processes to access with a patient is free association. Not interrupting the flow of a patient's free association process is one of my top priorities. This means that, if in the middle of a flow, a patient asks me a personal question that I would normally not answer or deflect, I might decide to answer, for the sake of preserving the flow. I will still, of course, wonder why the patient wants to know where I went on vacation or if I have children. When a patient is not in flow, I might pause and ask them about the impulse behind the question. As much as a patient may think they want to know a bit of personal information, it can be overstimulating. One of the crafts of my work is to assess whether a patient can handle the answer. Why have they asked? What is their fantasy around the answer? But, above all, I ask myself, what is the most important goal at this moment? If that goal is the flow, I may privilege its continuation and answer the question—depending upon the question.

5. My Socratic method. As I've mentioned, I am influenced by all the lawyers in my family and among my friends. Even when I think I already know the answer to a question, I know how much more valuable it is for the patient to arrive at the answer themselves. So I ask what may feel to me to be leading questions, posed as if they are completely open-ended. My aim is to lead my patient (yes!) to the awareness that is at the edge of

their consciousness. I am, in a sense, building a case on my patient's behalf, knowing that this bit of awareness will lead to an important conclusion. Unlike a lawyer, though, I am utterly comfortable not getting the answer I expect. It rarely happens, but when my leading questions yield an unexpected answer, the new insight is always interesting and important. I ask in the spirit of being open to pivoting in an unexpected direction, including continuing in the direction of not knowing the answer, or at least not knowing it at that time.

6. Answer questions, if only to explain why it would be better to not answer the question or not answer it at that time. It feels rude to answer a question with silence.

7. Caring is critical to change. Do not hide my warmth, yet be restrained in the expression of it.

8. You must want to heal others, a whole lot.

9. Developing theories about the patient and a strong intellectual backing is critical.

10. Be both a scientist and an artist in the work.

11. Offer psycho-ed. I have started giving some patients insights into the process and theory of therapy. I may explain, for example, why it's better I don't answer a question. I may explain what we can learn from various random thoughts that a patient is holding back, because she fears the thoughts are silly or trivial, or the relevance of a patient's past in understanding their present. Patients can often benefit from some education about the psychological landscape they are navigating.

12. Offer the occasional life philosophy. Many of my patients now talk about feeling meaningless and despairing in the face of the pandemic. I say, "Well, a lot of this has to do with what everyone is going

through. We're all living through this trauma and I don't think we will know how we were all affected until afterward." Whereas the norm is to make everything particular to the patient, with this statement, I normalize their despair, using a more general *we* than I would under usual circumstances.

None of these attitudes or theories are unique to me—other therapists are drawing on these same ideas in their own personalized ways. At a certain point, these personal theories also blend with the formal theories I've studied over the years. I am actively engaged in a process of getting in closer, more intentional touch with the ways my life outside of my training informs my technique so that I can offer my patients the best possible presence, support, and healing environment in our work together.

CHAPTER FOUR

Virtual Therapy (Really!) Works but Doesn't Substitute for In-Person. What's the Balance?

I've mentioned it throughout this book, but here I want to take a few pages to specially note the efficacy and depth of healing that I've discovered is possible in virtual therapy. Despite all that is unsettling and the difficulties bridging the distance, virtual is better than nothing, and the work of therapy continues to be deep and productive.

Linda, a willowy, attractive woman in her mid-fifties, says to me, "I am so happy about COVID. I don't know if I would be here without it." For a woman with a sunny, kind, and sensitive disposition, she is in an exceptionally bright mood for our phone session. Linda has spent months completely alone in her new, post-divorce house. She has lots of friends and relatives she meets up with virtually, and recently she has started going to work at her office and out to do some socially distanced, outdoor socializing. She is an avid tennis player and happy to be back on the court. But today, she is particularly happy, not only because she is chatting with an interesting man she met on a dating app—her first since her divorce—and not only because her twin daughters have told her how deeply they respect her strength, through all the difficulties of the divorce, but because she feels so much better about herself. She is liking herself, maybe for the first time in a long time. She feels strong. She feels like she has choices and possibilities in her life. She is finding her voice.

As a therapist, I'm listening to what my patients tell me about what's happening and how they feel. Then it's my job to translate this information into what it signifies in their character development. The isolation and dark months of the pandemic prompted her to reach deep within herself and do some bitter, but eye-opening, soul searching. We spent a lot of our time together uncovering the meaning in her discoveries. The process enabled her to write her ex an email in which she finally spoke her truth to him, plainly and directly. For the first time ever, he apologized and took responsibility for his part of their problems, for blaming his own demons. This opened the way for us to look at how and why she had developed a poor opinion of herself. Before he died, for example, her father used to criticize her for her difficulties with English class in high school. She transferred that dynamic of insufficiency into her relationship with her husband. She made him the authority on her attractiveness, desirability, and intelligence—really, on her overall worth as a woman. Her husband's negative comments about her physique and sexual performance had sent her self-esteem plummeting. She had begun to transfer that same insecurity on to her new beau, until I challenged her. Did she truly believe that her new beau's slow response to one of her texts was because he didn't like her body? She was able to see how she was once again revisiting her tendency to make others the authority on her attractiveness or intelligence.

Now Linda says she feels attractive and optimistic about life and dating. She wants to do more dating. She wants to have sex, for the first time in many years!

In spite of Linda's vulnerabilities, she has been able to use her strength to heal herself. Prior to our work, she used her strength to put up with the hardships she suffered in a love-starved marriage. Her strength enabled her to profit from the trying circumstances of the pandemic and telephone work.

The word *astounding* belongs here. I have colleagues who have noted the same thing. The work of therapy has been working astoundingly well. I have colleagues who will never or will infrequently go back to their offices. Even patients who are struggling with not being with me in person are having rich and productive sessions. Sometimes I wonder whether the work is even deeper now. I don't think so. I just think I'm amazed by how good it can be. I don't know why that is. I wonder, am I working harder to compensate for the distance? Is there something about our faces being so close together on our screens? Is there something about the distance that promotes more self-disclosure and reflection on the patient's part? I don't have a definitive answer yet.

Then there's Thursday, October 15, 2020. I have one of my best days of clinical work ever. I have six patient sessions that yield startling and hugely impactful insights related to deep, hard-to-reach, sensitive topics that were hidden under protective layers. Grains of irritating psychic sand from which a pearl of precious insight emerges. My patients on this day include one new patient, four patients I've worked with for years, and one patient I've worked with for almost nineteen years. What does this say about working remotely and its losses? That we can do fruitful work in spite of the hardships. That patients can make great strides in remote work. Is it because the pandemic has forced them to go deeper to psychically survive (and they are up to that challenge!)? Is it a way in which I am more suggestive in my approach? Is it related to the virtuality or in spite of it? I have certainly facilitated patients' breakthroughs prior to the pandemic. Yet I am still surprised by my ability to facilitate the same progress remotely.

After numerous sessions of extreme ambivalence and overt resistance to the therapy process, punctuated with expressions of interest and cooperation, on this day Carol calls in, instead of her usual Zoom. The phone eases the way for her considerably. She is voluble and engaged. She talks about herself, asks questions and speaks about her experience of the therapy and the feeling of being freed up by the phone (versus Zoom). Her entire emotional tone is brighter. Later that day, she sends me that email I mentioned early in the book, filling me in on some important and highly personal background in her life.

Emma is sliding into a depression. Emma has it about as good as anyone does in life. She has considerable financial means; a long, warm, and devoted marriage; lovely children and grandchildren; excellent friends and family relationships, as well as several interesting careers under her belt. But Emma has been experiencing some significant hardship with one of her children, in addition to the hardship we have all been subjected to in

2020. Now her golden years are not looking so golden, and she is warding off despair. Depression is an unfamiliar state for her, one that she actively fights off with a positive attitude about life. It takes a lot for her to face her depression. She is one of the more realistic people I know, and she is a thinker—about life, politics, and society. She sees what is going on in our country, culture, government, and pandemic with a certain vision and clarity. She doesn't see the pandemic ending anytime soon and wonders what her remaining years will be like. Certainly not what she had planned and hoped for.

I know that Emma needs to face these pessimistic views and her depression, to find her way through to the other side. After deeply exploring her situation, reactions, and feelings, including the personal meaning of it all, I tell her that while I am hesitant to offer her such specific advice, because it could backfire, I tell her it is time for me to really prod her to do something for herself, to help her find meaning and purpose, as well as a measure of peace.

Emma is an empathic person. She gets enormous satisfaction out of caring for others, which simultaneously offers her redemption for a past tragedy. But her emotional bank account is overdrawn now. I start by telling her this. She knows it's true, so this is not a hard sell. I tell her that she would do well for herself to replenish the account by finding something meaningful for herself. We both know that for Emma, this could mean not only painting but finding a painting instructor to work with. One of the things that she needs is to increase her contact with others. I tell her that part of her despair emanates from her diminished contact with many of the people who give her joy. Disproving my fears that she will chafe under my suggestions, she is cheered, as if a light peeped into a dark and shadowy room.

After almost twenty years of working with Frank, I realize, on this same fruitful day, that so much of his copious anxiety relates to feeling dominated by his three older siblings, a pattern that replays in his current relationship with his wife. His reaction to feeling pressured is to turn up his volume and sound aggressive and dictatorial. In other words, underneath his imposing behavior is anxiety and insecurity, a fear of being steamrolled and dismissed.

I see Finn this day, too. Finn's wife is usually in his dreams. Recently she has been missing from them. We explore why this big shift is happening in his unconscious. Late in our hardworking session, we discover that his wife represents his life span. At age sixty-seven, he has known her for most of his life. They have been a couple since high school. Finn's wife provided him with great love and a home, both literal and psychic. She rescued him from a sense of lovelessness and feelings of exclusion in his life. Both have tasted a sliver of their mortality through their own and each other's illnesses and recovery. Finn has gotten a peek at the end of the road. What will happen when his wife (his life) is no longer there? We realize that the ubiquitous images of cars in his dreams represent the engine that drives him through life. He wonders whether he can drive alone if his wife dies first. This scenario is so painful that it first presents itself in the disguised form of a dream. Finn's persistent curiosity about his mental life allows the fear to rise up to his consciousness through our work together.

The Hayes, a family of five, are also on my schedule for the day. The father starts out the session with a concern about his son. His son is not cleaning his room. The father speaking first is atypical. In fact, his is the main voice of the whole session. His son, who usually protects his father (a man who normally can do no wrong in his eyes), gets activated and cries out, "You hurt me." He points out all the ways he has become more responsible for himself, and he asks his parents to stay out of his room, his life, and his self-care. He says he can handle it on his own terms. After suffering a major depression, this new attitude is an accomplishment. His mother steps in briefly, to say that the father also scolds her for house clutter. The brevity of the mother's participation is atypical for her. The father, normally restrained, sitting in on the sidelines, protected from the family drama, says, "You two are so emotional."

Here we reap the fruit of many months of work. I point out that after stepping into the family drama for possibly the first time, he has pushed all the emotion in the room off on his wife and son. Even though he clearly has strong feelings. I explain that his son was set off by his intrusiveness and covert criticism, not seeing the son's recent great strides in being more independently responsible for himself. The son calms down in response to this intervention. I encourage his father to continue with his closeted feelings. He is emboldened, expressing the emotions that lie behind his worry, his fears that the messy room would cloud the son's thinking process. In the process, he discovers the associations with the scarcity of the emotional life in his family of origin. He reveals that early in his life, he identified music as a way that he could connect to his passionate internal life. As a result of his opening to his own emotions, his wife can remove the target from her chest. She has always been the emotional center of the family. She is the one who does the heavy emotional lifting, particularly for the son's needs. This has made her the target of everyone's frustrations.

This session takes a big step toward putting each of their feelings and roles in their proper baskets. The father's instrument has finally started playing in the family's emotional orchestra. The mother section quiets. The son section fades out softly.

After a difficult beginning, Ellie gets to the heart of what troubles her—her ambivalence. Difficult beginnings are typical with Ellie, though less and less so. In this session we get some insight into this difficulty via her ambivalence. In psychoanalytic terms, ambivalence is a state of being, like anger or anxiety. Ellie is ambivalent about many things. Today, instead of locating her indecisiveness in external circumstances, for the first time, she locates the ambivalence inside herself. This insight will help her see how elements of her dissatisfaction reside within, rather than because of others' actions. This will allow her to look into what she can change in herself. We connect this ambivalence to many aspects of her life. This realization, something that we have been working toward for a very long time, is a big milestone. We have opened the door to the next big stage of therapeutic work. Why and what shrouded, ancient experiences inside Ellie drive this ambivalence? This is a painful place to reach. I recognize that surfacing this new understanding, at long last, likely accounts for some of her difficulty in beginning sessions.

Sometimes the most challenging work with the most resistant patients can yield rich results because the patient's resistance leads them to engage vigorously and authentically with the therapy. In addition, I'm beginning to think that the changed and challenging circumstances are causing an intense focus in the work of therapy, which is yielding rich and productive outcomes for those who stick with it.

October 15, 2020, was quite a day!

CHAPTER FIVE

How Are We? . . . Where Are We and Where Are We Going Post-Pandemic?

There was life before the pandemic, life during, and in the coming months there will be life after the pandemic. *After* the pandemic we will return to an updated version of normal. It will be the same as the old normal in some ways, and new and different in other ways. In the same way that a couple of millennia ago the world moved from BC to AD and much was the same, yet there were also new and important shifts.

As a massive vaccination initiative rolls out across the country and the world, we begin a new period of history. Even as we bore the fresh scars of the pandemic, we welcomed the new Biden-Harris administration and the end of the Trump presidency and all that entailed with its lies and violence and insurrection. If history and the Spanish flu pandemic of 1918–1919 provide any lesson, it's that we will return to an updated version of normal life. At the same time, some changes are permanent—at least until the next big watershed event.

Two forces of change strike me in particular. The first and most profound is a radical shift to the non-physical world of the internet. We were already more focused on cyber work and communication and less on the world of place and physical objects, like newspapers and shopping. The pandemic catalyzed that process.

The second force has to do with the particularities of the American pandemic experience, which was so colored by the most chaotic and authoritarian administration in American history that it was almost impossible to separate the two. Listening to my patients and experiencing my own responses, I heard how the two experiences intermingled in people's hearts and minds, how a large swath of the country went through the parallel traumas of the pandemic and the corrupt and uncaring administration of Donald Trump.

What would it have been like to go through the pandemic with strong leadership? With leadership that inspired confidence and hope? With a leadership that was empathic to the plights of all Americans? President Biden gave us a glimpse as he steered us through the last treacherous waters of the pandemic. If the pandemic had been the only threat, we might not have felt so besieged.

For me (and I imagine a group of my patients, who seemed just as spooked as me), the experience of the election was like waiting for the outcome of a potential cancer surgery with all the attendant sick feelings and inability to think of anything else. I've been there, too. First you wait for the surgeon's impression of the tumor from the diagnostic surgery he just performed. Then you wait for the path report. You dread the possibility of cancer. If it is going to be cancer, you hope for an optimistic prognosis with a viable treatment plan. You imagine a terminal diagnosis. We waited for the outcome with that same sense of doom.

As Americans, we are not used to our viability being threatened right here on our soil. The Trump administration's lack of a coherent response to the pandemic, the attack on the Capitol, and the near collapse of our democracy exposed vulnerabilities to our existence as a nation as we know it. Reckoning with that legacy will be an extended process.

Meanwhile, the pandemic raged on and many more people died during the course of the Trump administration than had to die. Sometimes tragedies are so big that putting them into words seems minimizing. In addition to the deaths, there were the devastating losses of income and the yawning gap of income inequality unmasked. A daunting challenge at the top of President Biden's agenda.

I did not experience the loss of a loved one or a catastrophic loss of income. My husband and I have experienced some loss of income, but not major, and we were okay. And there were silver linings. Paradoxically, the period of distance and remoteness presented opportunities for new or renewed closeness with friends. We found comfort in each other's company during a period of privation and anxiety. We went to great lengths to meet friends in our backyards as it got colder, often sitting around our firepit and shivering as a small price to pay for each other's company. We let down our guard in ways we hadn't before because we could not escape our human vulnerabilities.

We were all susceptible to sickness and death. We continue to carry this heightened awareness around with us.

Sadly, strangely, interestingly, there are things about the pandemic world that I miss. I want to be wise enough to capture what they are, to name them and savor them, because I know that even if I manage to hold on to a piece of them, as we get further away from the pandemic, many will ebb away.

I loved staying home. My life prior to the pandemic was frenetic. I could not figure out how to change it without feeling that it would involve too much of a sacrifice. I loved being able to flow fluidly in my house, between meeting with patients, writing, exercise, domestic duties, mealtime, back and forth, back and forth. I wrote this book with that same fluidity in mind, interweaving observations of my therapy practice and my personal journey, thinking about how the different aspects of myself, personal and professional, make sense together, like interlocking puzzle pieces.

Life was simpler and very outdoorsy for me. Society doesn't only fill needs. It creates needs. More than a year after traversing the long, dark tunnel of the pandemic, I am standing in the light of the beginning of the end. I see how bloated my life before had become. I feel lighter now and dread the inevitable revival of activities and re-accumulation of objects. I thought I had locked away my beautiful engagement ring for the duration of the pandemic. I felt freer and less in need of valuable material objects, even this one which I adored for its beauty and sentimental value. One year later I discovered I had actually lost it. I was devastated, as if I had lost a beloved person. I felt punished for trying to liberate myself from the burden of caring for something, even though I'd put my ring in what I thought was a secure place—the trusted hands of our safe. I had inadvertently traded the responsibility that comes with material possessions for the emotional cost of loss. There are tradeoffs with all choices and we can't always know what they are in advance.

Had I not been pulled into this lifestyle by the currents of the pandemic, I would have remained more rooted in my city life. Yet, I loved, still love, and will (I hope) continue to love my brisk walks and long, cold bike rides, surrounded by the smell of fires, my get-togethers around the firepit eating s'mores and drinking hot apple cider, and cozy evenings on the couch swathed in comfortable clothes and, of course, my Bombas socks. I have become hardier and am getting deep satisfaction out of testing myself against this more bracing style of life. These are changes I will not give up. Prior to the pandemic, I was cosseted by the services that I outsourced to satisfy my needs, such as my well-supplied gym with its spa, if I wanted a massage; instant help when anything broke down in my home; and the smoothing effects of hair, skin and nail care. During the pandemic, I cooked (or at least foraged for food while straining to get my workload managed), cleaned, schlepped logs and made fires, enjoyed a greatly reduced wardrobe range, colored my roots, filed my nails, and so on. I liked a lot of aspects of this challenge.

My new normal will be modified. I will go back to restaurants with a vengeance, but I will not get my nails done regularly. I will color my hair myself but go to a salon for occasional highlights. Prior to the pandemic, I was already trending toward a dislike of cocktail gatherings and big parties. Going forward, I will respect my internal compass, which generally points to small gatherings. The pandemic released me from my need to be a polished host. Potluck or a big bowl of simple spaghetti appeals to me in a way it never did before. And movies. To sit in a theater surrounded by others, watching the same big-screen, cinematic story with me—wonderful!

Another aspect of my cocooning pleasure was the well-feathered nest I took care to design. My home expresses my creativity in its comfort, beauty, and user-friendly environment. I derive a deep satisfaction from being able to provide for myself, which I didn't have in my home growing up. I had no say over my environment (even my room). There were too many bare floors. I was often cold, with no say over the thermostat. Rooms were not set up for good working conditions or privacy or a comfortable place to relax, with or without others. I felt so lucky during the pandemic to have a space that nurtured and fit me.

The newfound pleasures of home life come with a measure of guilt. Full disclosure—during the pandemic I reduced my patient hours slightly in order to allow myself time to reboot and refresh from the fatigue of virtual work. I know that I will never go all the way back to the punishing schedule and life structure that I maintained before the pandemic. I feel guilt not only about the pleasure of cocooning, but about the specific pleasure around the regressive aspect of cozying up at home with all these little pockets of extra time that have been freed up by not commuting or going anywhere at all. I feel guilty about how much I'm savoring the womb-like feelings of drawing inward, the amount of time I spend watching Netflix, reading, and listening to podcasts.

My guilt relates to an experience I share with my patient Rosemary. Often (not always) the kind of drive to succeed and achieve, which provokes my guilt, can relate to an uneasy sense that to let go is not safe. There is no one minding the parental store, and I must be my own parent. A feeling that I am all alone in the effort to handle the chores of life. Such people (me?!) can become very capable and not even realize how much we take on because it is second nature. For Rosemary and me, our parents were absorbed in their own insistent needs and worries, leaving them less available for the rest of the family's needs. When that happens, it can leave people like Rosemary and myself with unfinished longings to lie on a hammock and while the afternoon away with a book or a journey inside our imagination—longings that feel forbidden.

So it's no wonder that it took time for me to relax into the cocooned state of working and living the pandemic forced upon us. Somewhere around the eighth month of the pandemic, the sand timer in my head that was always threatening to run out of time stopped its unsettling cascade of sand grains. Though I still feel self-indulgent, I have grown comfortable living without the usual urgency that marked my life before. At some point the sand grains will start to flow again, marking time, but never with as much speed as they did before the pandemic. I have tasted from the tree of knowledge of a different lifestyle, and it is too sweet to give it up altogether. This is an example of a regression that can be adaptive, especially if it is accompanied by a sense of mindful choice, a recognition of the necessity and opportunity in turning inward.

I know others who share my sentiments about giving up the cocooned pandemic lifestyle, now that it is drawing to a close. While I would like to regain certain discrete losses, I feel some dread about going out into the world again, at least at the same pace as I had before the pandemic. Is this a return of the familiar separation anxiety that has dogged me my whole life? Is this a healthy, more balanced correction of that compulsive aspect of me, always driven to accomplish one more task, one more errand, one more manicure that otherwise might get away from me? How long can I retain at least a portion of this calmer, simpler, earthier, less harried lifestyle that offers more opportunities for quiet contemplation than before the plague?

I must also recognize that some small part of what felt so compelling in the hibernation is, in all likelihood, an expression of mourning. How could I not sorely miss some elements of my life? I enjoyed many aspects of life pre-pandemic. How could they vanish without some sadness and mourning? I also fell prey to the anxiety that comes from not knowing when the crisis would end, the very same anxiety felt by most of my patients. Even now, I wonder whether my son's wedding, now scheduled for spring 2022, will actually come to pass. When will I be able to travel to the list of exotic countries on my bucket list? As I write that, I recognize that my desire to travel has changed. I am no longer as tempted by foreign destinations. I am relishing the idea of getting to know the United States better. We all share this continued uncertainty. Mourning comes in waves. I am mourning, even as I am experiencing new pleasures. My vitality is undiminished.

And what of the physical space of my work, the safe haven of the therapist's consulting room coupled with the human configuration of two people engaged face-to-face, speaking their hearts and minds freely and confidentially, one searching and the other guiding? There are losses. And there are gains. As with all change, which may be progress, simply opposing the new with no idea of accommodation or alternative only serves to keep us out of touch and frustrated. Virtual work, including phone and internet, is here to stay. As the pandemic ends, our lives will fill up again with a bewildering array of choices. We have bitten from the apple of alternative work and meeting arrangements, and there is no going back to a rigid system.

Ever the moderate, I favor a hybrid system, where I and my patients take advantage of the convenience of remote therapy for some number of sessions per month, plus some in-person meetings, so as not to lose the irreplaceable human element of being in the same room together. Often my mind wanders to that day when my patients and I get to experience the full spectrum of human presence without masks. We gain a huge amount of information about people unconsciously, through smell, for example, and we can go into a depression without that very sense that so many people have been deprived of when stricken by COVID. Talk about appreciating a sense that we all took for granted pre-pandemic. I speak to as many people who miss the office, as I do to those who could kiss it goodbye. In particular, people who rely on the office for an important venue of social contact as well as an avenue to make themselves known for promotions and desired work assignments.

My guess is that there will be lots of coworking office spaces at different levels of cost and amenities, in which people will share, borrow, and rent space that they can use when they need and want to go to a physical space. Where and how will people meet? What do we do about loneliness and the practical human problem of losing what gets transmitted only by being with a person in the flesh? These questions and dilemmas will affect arrangements for therapy offices. Consistency, familiarity, and routine have been linchpins of therapy practice. The solid foundation upon which trust can be built. If therapists use coworking offices, how will that affect the therapy atmosphere?

I have noticed that peoples' preferences for going back to the office versus staying home, divide into roughly two groups (there are undoubtedly other categories but these are the two that strike me). Younger adults whose home spaces may be small and cramped, are eager to get back to the office for the space. They tend to depend on their work environment as an important source of social life and meeting people. Whereas, for many of us who are more seasoned and have found partners, had children, and had more time to build social networks, we continue to relish the opportunity to turn inward.

As the vaccines roll out, I ask myself, how I will preserve even a fragment of this peace when it's over? What residue of this new life will remain when the tide goes out and we roll back into a more normalized life? I am determined to use the pandemic reset as an opportunity to reconsider, reshuffle the deck, and have the courage to institute transformative changes in my own life and the way I work.

Our world in general, the profession of therapy in particular, and my individual life (and yours!) will be filled with an array of choices. We've been moving in that direction in steady increments over the past few decades. As women we can choose to wear long or short dresses, or pants. We can choose whether to marry, whom we want to marry, and how we want to have children. If we are fortunate enough that our finances don't compel us to get a paycheck, we can even choose whether we want to be employed or not. We were already heading down a virtual path. The pandemic has paved and widened that path into a highway, giving us yet more choices. We will be able to choose whether and when to go into the office; what kind of office; how we are meeting, if not in the office; and what kind of platform. These choices will give rise to other choices. Since we will no longer be chained to a physical office space, we may be able to choose what locale we want to be living in and for how long. These choices will reverberate into yet more choices, as the whole landscape shifts. Should we choose to recognize this breadth of choice, we may feel a greater sense of agency in sculpting our lifestyle to better fit our own needs.

Let me finish my thoughts with the topic of pleasure. After all, the very goal of therapy is to allow people to feel more fulfilled in their lives, to derive greater pleasure from *what is* as opposed to what you think should be. Precious energy is wasted on fighting something that is beyond our control. It has always been true that we must take our pleasure where we can find it. In the wake of the pandemic, that adage feels truer now than ever. Many people have difficulty taking pleasure knowing that others are suffering. They feel guilty. After much of a lifetime of that guilt, I have learned to take my pleasure where I can find it. I find it in my work with patients, my family and friends, my writing, alone time, good food, reading, exercise, and, of course, cocooning, to name a few! The point is, whether we like it or not, the pandemic happened and will continue to impact our lives for some time to come. But we still have choices about how we meet this circumstance and how we adapt. Ask yourself what you can get out of the pandemic. For me, there has been a longed-for return to a simplified, pared down lifestyle, with a greater concentration on the basics of daily living. What insights into your own preferences and desires did the pandemic offer?

Did you always want to spend more time at home, alone or with family? What the pandemic made clear to me is that if we can accept that the pandemic just is, and that we were not entitled to a life without a pandemic, we may find that alongside our sadness, frustration, and anger are small and large opportunities for pleasure. One day at a time.

Epilogue

M other's Day, 2021. My family and I, my friends, and most of my patients are all lucky enough to have been vaccinated. For the first time since March 2020, I had the luxury of my whole family inside the house for dinner. No masks! More than just Mother's Day, we were celebrating the slow reopening of our country. There is still a ways to go.

As my husband and I try to figure out our office space, for when we "go back," we keep looking to the future as if it has a start date. We are in the future now, riddled with uncertainty as it is. Will we go back to an outside office gradually, all at once, or in a hybrid form? One of our big questions is whether we can combine our offices. My husband and I are in very different professions. Will my patients be uncomfortable crossing paths with his business appointments or will they accept the situation as a new normal?

Uncertainty characterizes this moment. Can we go with the flow? Make our decisions with the current? Resist the urge to force certainty where none can exist? We must treat our best decision about office space as an experiment. Give ourselves flexibility and make the most of it. As much as we seek certainty, often certainty is an illusion. The good news is that periods of flux give rise to growth, creativity, and solutions. I am nervous and excited. And *tired*. We all want answers.

I'm blinking in the light of day as I come out of hibernation. Seeing people feels unnerving and energizing. I loved the freedom of not wearing makeup. Seeing people in person again tugs on the old vanity. I put on mascara. Not every day as in pre-pandemic times. I've changed. We've all changed. We've tasted the freedom to be different. We got permission to appreciate how variety and flexibility add spice to life. Freedom is hybrid.

Scientists say that infection rates will go way down and ultimately will be brought under control, similar to the occasional measles outbreaks. They also say that we are unlikely to reach *herd immunity* for another two generations. We will have significant improvement, but not the total release we had hoped for with the vaccines. We can still live full and meaningful lives. We just have to adapt to the uncertainty and precautions. We adjust to new lenses and see that we will have ongoing opportunities to make change in our lives.

The decisions we make during this period of reopening and transition come with *anxiety*. A small minority of my patients and several new referrals want to be seen in person, as soon as I am willing. Though not exclusively, they tend to be young adults. What irony! The generation growing up online yearns for the physical presence of their therapist. I am so glad that human presence still matters to them. I am thinking hard about what this need means and how I can find a way to honor it. I am not yet ready to go back to the office. On the other hand, I may need to be more flexible around my expectations for practicing therapy. Maybe I can adapt to wearing a mask during a patient session and taking their temperature when they arrive. There is no single correct answer. I am checking in with my evolving values, my thoughts, feelings, and needs. The answer will present itself. Having weathered the radical shift to all virtual therapy, I know that I have built the muscle to cope with this new adjustment.

We all face decisions about space. Depending on who we are, we may want more or less contact with others. We may be facing pressure to go into work before we are ready. We may have friends who want to gather indoors before we are ready. We may have children who have been suffering the loss of school in person. New norms are developing as I write this.

Helping to plan my son's wedding for next year, I have to include the possibility that the plans will change . . . again. Just like inclement weather, I'll plan for inclement health conditions. We are all coming to terms with what is right for us, within the context of our values, needs, and wants, and making decisions accordingly. The pandemic has driven home to me that our lives are not a dress rehearsal for a show happening tomorrow. At the same time, the enormous changes I have learned to live with over the past many months have been an important rehearsal for the adaptability I need to cultivate, to deal with ongoing changes I will be faced with, as the future unfolds.

How do we want to live right now, with all the risks, limits, and new freedoms? How can we accept and embrace the idea that what I choose now may need an adjustment tomorrow? And that it's ok.

I am reminded that we should be good and compassionate with ourselves. To not require perfection in our choices or our circumstances. We don't have all the answers right now in this moment. I have permission to practice therapy differently and to readjust as I feel necessary. The pandemic has taught us that there is always an opportunity to make change. That's what learning is.